MAN MADE PERFECT

MAN MADE PERFECT

The Science of Spiritual Evolution

Teachings from
The White Brotherhood
transmitted to

MABEL BEATTY

PELEGRIN TRUST
in association with
PILGRIM BOOKS
TASBURGH · NORWICH · ENGLAND

First published 1929
by Rider & Co
Reproduced for this edition 1987

British Library Cataloguing in Publication Data
Man made perfect: the science of spiritual evolution.
1. Spirit writings
I. Beatty, Mabel   II. White, Brotherhood
133.9′3   BF1301
ISBN 0–946259–22–4

Printed in Great Britain
at the University Printing House, Oxford
by David Stanford
Printer to the University

FOREWORD

THIS is in no sense a book of personal opinions, nor had I been associated with Spiritualism in any form until quite unexpectedly I received a message through a psychic friend by means of planchette that I was to try to write myself.

I had no desire to do so, and had no knowledge that one could receive anything of a serious nature through automatic writing. I regarded planchette and all such methods as rather stupid forms of amusement.

However, I had been impressed with other evidence received through this friend, so thought I would try.

In July, 1926, I began to experiment with pencil and paper and had a few results, and on September 9th, 1926, I received through my own hand the intimation by some influence purporting to be a Guide that after I had written a novel I was to be used for writing a book of mystical teachings.

This novel was not even written at that time but is now published, all having happened exactly as foretold.

As I became more and more fluent in automatic writing, I began to receive teachings of an outstanding quality on various subjects. These came in short paragraphs, sometimes in answer to questions ; there was no proper sequence in any of the material at that time.

On June 4th, 1928, I received this intimation : " We think it would be safe to start on this great work."

By this time it was obvious that there were several influences working through me. The writing varied, some was written with my left hand backwards, and each influence gave his own special symbol on coming through.

On September 2nd, 1928, the actual first complete paper on the number Four was given, after I had been specially bidden to write the matter on the numbers One, Two, and

FOREWORD

Three. I do not know why I was made do this. I protested in vain. Later I was made to write a short introduction to the section on Mystery Schools. With these two exceptions the whole of the script has been sent through by automatic writing.

During October, November, December, 1928, and January, 1929, owing to illness in my family I was obliged to give up writing, but on February 26th I began to receive the long papers which form the book as it stands now. The writing came quickly, fluently, and was on subjects unknown to me, often giving expression to ideas contrary to my own thoughts. This continued with short breaks until I received the final chapter on May 28th.

After several of these papers had been written I was told to submit them to a certain circle of friends and to invite them to ask questions. These were answered at once, and in their presence through me, often before I had had time to appreciate their tenour.

The White Brotherhood appears to be a body of high Guides through whom these writings have come, and I was told to send out this book under their auspices; the reason is obvious in their concluding chapter.

I have been conscious throughout my work of a wonderful fellowship; the personalities of these Spirit Friends, if I may use such a term, have been as real as the physical presence of my earthly friends, and their companionship a comfort and an inspiration.

I have never undertaken any portion of this work whether by myself or in my circle without prayer for guidance and for protection in the Name of our Lord Jesus Christ; and in His Name and in the name of my Brethren in the House of Remembrance I send this into the world, trusting that the peace which has entered my own heart may enter the hearts of many others.

MABEL BEATTY.

September 4th, 1929.

PREFACE

This edition is published by the Pelegrin Trust, a registered charity which exists for the publication or re-publication of books considered to be of spiritual worth.

Man Made Perfect was first published in 1929. In re-publishing almost sixty years after the material was received, the Trust is conscious that a few passages may be seen to reflect opinions or attitudes current at that time which may now be unacceptable. In any mediumistic communication a clear channel cannot be guaranteed at all times; it may be considered that such passages are attributable more to the mind of the medium than to the communicators.

CONTENTS

CHAPTER IV

CHAPTER V

CHAPTER VI

CHAPTER VII

CHAPTER VIII

CHAPTER IX

CHAPTER X

CONTENTS

CHAPTER XI

PART II

MAN

CHAPTER XII

CHAPTER XIII

CHAPTER XIV

CHAPTER XV

CHAPTER XVI

CHAPTER XVII

CHAPTER XVIII

CHAPTER XIX

CHAPTER XX

PART III

THE NEW FAITH

CHAPTER XXI

CHAPTER XXII

CHAPTER XXIII

CHAPTER XXIV

CHAPTER XXV

CHAPTER XXVI

CHAPTER XXVII

CHAPTER XXVIII

PART I

COSMOS

" In the beginning God created "

CHAPTER I

THE SPIRITUAL SIGNIFICANCE OF NUMBERS

ONE. The first Cause. The Point within the Circle. The All-Seeing Eye.
Two. Law of Duality. Law of Affinities. Sex.
THREE. Manifestation. The Trinitarian Concept.

THE science of number or numbers must necessarily form the basis of all religious thought, all attempts to render thought intelligible being entirely impossible apart from its consideration.

Whether regarded as a series of digits added together to convey a sense of principles, or as a series of geometrical figures used to convey a conception of form, is immaterial ; the great underlying idea or the scaffolding on which knowledge is built up depends on the putting into motion in vibratory wave-lengths of universal, subtle material (which we call mind) a terminology, or a set of terms, which will give us abstract ideas in concrete language : which will give us the reason, as it were, for our own existing world in material form.

We cannot move in any plane of consciousness, we cannot express life or thought without involuntarily calling into existence some expression of that science which is universal in exposition and symbol, the science of numerology or numbers.

" In the beginning "—What beginning ? What do we mean by a beginning ? We know perfectly well that in order to have a history of life, a collection of forms, a series of coherent ideas, we have to go back to something which we call a beginning : some one cause which effected this vast structure, which we call the universe, or, to bring it down to the everyday commonplace, this wonderful creation which we call our earth.

The beginning can only be expressed by a point, a centre,

something having all things potential in itself, yet in its essence something which is expressed by ONE.

ONE.

Life emanated from a true unity, a real one-ness ; it could not have emanated from negation, or from anything lacking entire agreement with itself, therefore in all schools of thought, in all degrees of scientific exposition, in all cults and religions there is, and can only be, a single universal symbol known as ONE.

Though it may be expressed as the point within the circle, the all-seeing eye, or the monad, it is that expression of the unknowable Cause of all life in all planes within our own limited powers of consciousness and beyond.

We can hardly say that ONE stands for God, for God as First Cause is altogether beyond our comprehension however we may try to talk about Him as God the Father, for even to talk of Him as such limits the Illimitable.

God the Father and the First Great Cause of all cannot be the same. But as we cannot hope to get within even measurable understanding of what God is, still less the First Great Cause, let us agree to accept a working hypothesis by which we may, as it were, take God for granted as the highest possible idea of Being and Reality, standing as a great and grand Principle in the symbol of I AM or ONE. We shall still find ourselves vaguely aware of an immeasurably lofty degree of consciousness to which we can only aspire in great, albeit rare, moments of worship and inner communion, but through the symbol or number ONE we shall be enabled to express God to ourselves by putting a limit to Him, the limit of the symbol ONE.

ONE, therefore, as far as we can understand it, expresses Being, Existence, Unity, and as the root of all things, ideas, ideals, as the essence of life and form, ONE expresses the ideas and ideal of Unity.

For the moment we will leave the number ONE with its outstanding meaning of Unity, with all that it can teach us of our relationship to God and pass on by natural sequence to the analysis of the other numbers.

Two.

When our minds have established the number ONE as a symbol of being in the abstract, then instinctively we can fathom the meaning of the next number.

" From the One sprang the Two." The great division of God emanating from a great desire.

In the number TWO we are given the law of Duality, the law of Affinities, the law of Polarity.

Herein do we meet a law which appears on the surface to be a paradox. Division, which is a breaking apart from, a halving, a placing of a barrier, an introducing of an opposition, is yet a law of affinity.

Yet we understand immediately the necessity for the division, because thought or realization cannot become possible without it. The abstract must become concrete. We cannot entertain the simple ideas of heat, light, male, positive, fast, unless we can imagine conditions of cold, darkness, female, negative, slow.

To our finite understanding, that which is neither hot nor cold, light nor dark, fast nor slow, is negative and indicative of stagnation ; so that TWO is also necessarily the number of discrimination and of progress. It is also the number which expresses affinity.

The law of Affinities is a deep mystery, far beyond the fact that it is a scientific reality. It is the spiritual law of Sex, a law greatly misunderstood and much abused. The history, spiritual, mental, and physical, of our world is entirely dependent on, wrapped up in and evolved out of, the great law of Sex, which is expressed variously in such terms as male and female, attraction'and repulsion, centripetal and centrifugal, positive and negative.

Only the gross materialism of Man has degraded that divine law into a law of the jungle, a law of gratification, of animal appetites, and made it a subject of cheap sentiment, or even worse, an object of disgusting cynicism. That is because of his ignorance, his misunderstanding of his divine origin. We have heard too much of the ape, and too little of Man's being made in the image of God, too much of the " miserable sinner," too little of the time when in close spiritual partnership, he walked and talked with God.

Yet it is possible to think of the ONE, that great creative Being, in an impulse of divine desire rending Itself in twain, and at that impulse becoming the systole and diastole of the Cosmic Heart, the symbol of eternal love, quite possible to conceive of perpetual rhythm becoming a law of the unborn universe.

These are ideas from a wider, fuller consciousness towards which Man's imagination can guide him, a fuller consciousness open to all lovers ; it is no idle dream that poets write of Love Immortal, or that the Mystic speaks of Love Transcendental : Love is a grand cosmic truth and the number TWO is its universal symbol.

THREE.

By a natural sequence of ideas we pass to the number THREE, the number of Manifestation.

There is no number so pregnant with divine and universal suggestion as this number, and its importance to us as a principle in cosmic and human law can be quickly seen, for it pervades all planes of mental conceptions, all degrees of matter. It is the number of Birth, that which issuing from the union of the TWO gives the symbol of the Son, of Divine or Perfect Manhood.

Through the Union of the Opposites we perceive the third Principle, that of Vitalisation, that is the direction of energy. These are cosmic factors on which all life depends.

The religious history of the world is permeated with the trinitarian idea. We have only to remember the trinities of Osiris, Isis, and Horus in Egypt ; Brahma, Vishnu, and Shiva in India ; Anu, Hea, and Bel in Chaldea. In Jewish Kabbalism we find the three great Sephiroth, Kether (the crown), Chochmah (wisdom), and Binah (understanding) ; among the ancient Druids, Aesar, Anu Mathar, and Ain ; in Freemasonry, Solomom and the two Hirams, or the Master and his two Wardens. In Christianity we should have the trinity of Father-God, Mother-God, and Son-God, or Spirit-God.

Originally these agreed in function with the more cosmic presentment of general religious belief ; they became anthropomorphised later, when the feminine principle was discarded, the divine man Jesus promoted to a place in the trinity that should have been occupied in a spiritual sense by a state known as the Christ-Consciousness, for the underlying principles of all trinities have been those of Existence, i.e. I AM-ness ; Division or Desire, i.e. Thou Art-ness ; Manifestation, i.e. He Is-ness.

Creator or Divine Father ; Preserver or Divine Mother ; and Regenerator or Saviour, Divine Son.

Cosmic principles or truths are involved in all planes of existence, and we in our present physical state are seeing " through a glass darkly " the presentment of the trinity in our own human conditions and functions of father, mother, child. The realization of what such relationship stands for surely gives a dignity and a purpose to life little comprehended by man or woman. If it were, there would be no foolish idea of the inferiority of one sex ; and decency, honour, cleanliness would be the rule of domestic life rather than the present ignorance.

Leaving the purely physical, we have in wireless the transmitter, the receiver, and that which is collected, sent and made audible, i.e. manifestation through sound.

In colour, we have the union of two complementary colours producing something which nearly approaches white, and white we know contains all colours or manifestations of vibration through colour.

On the mental plane, the plane on which all human existence depends, we have the thinker, the act of thinking, and the thing thought of. In the constitution of man we have a body, a soul and a spirit.

Returning to fundamentals, we have the cosmic trinity of God, Man, and the Universe, expressed in varying term by Philosopher, Mystic, or Occultist, so that we know beyond all shadow of doubt that the number THREE becomes and remains a symbol universal and inevitable in every respect.

.   .   .   .   .

It was at this point that the writing was taken over by the various Guides, who have been entirely responsible for all the matter and wording given, with the small exception of my own short introduction to the chapter on Mystery Schools, which " they " insisted on my writing. I can give no explanation as to why any of these papers should have been written by me. Some of the ideas introduced by me have been written from thoughts inspired by sentences scattered throughout the many pages of script received automatically by my hand, so that, although to be strictly accurate throughout this book, I must inform the reader that two small portions out of this vast wealth of material were written in my own words, I am still indebted to the Great Ones, whose medium I have the honour to be, for the mental conceptions on which these words depend.

M. B.

CHAPTER II

THE SPIRITUAL SIGNIFICANCE OF NUMBERS (*contd.*)

FOUR. The Fourth Dimension. Extension of Consciousness. Levitation. The Number of Stability, Proportion, Rhythm, Building.
FIVE. The Five Senses. The Initiate. Man's Spiritual Responsibility. The Five-pointed Star.
SIX. The Number of Balance. Solomon's Seal. The Interlaced Triangles. The Number of Love. Love is Highest Wisdom. The Divine Fatherhood. The Six-pointed Star. The Six Points of Wisdom. Correspondences. Illusion. Reality. The Real Saviours. The Promise of the Future.

FOUR.

WHEN your mind tries to fathom the mysteries of the number FOUR, it struggles with the real mystery of what is known in your world as the fourth dimension, and of course it is very difficult to put into such terms as would be understood by the human mind, some special idea which has no part in its ordinary terms of speech ; for, of course, your mind attempts at once to make a very high contact, and there are no real three-dimensional terms which can in any measure express what such a space means.

Let us assume that when you speak of a dimension your brain fully understands what is meant by this term, for mankind has a very haphazard way of using words, often with little regard for their real sense.

The word means a certain rate of vibration between certain given points specified as between A and B, or between A, B, and C, but when your mind tries to go a step further and wishes to give some measurement for some figure which needs a fourth letter, then it gets quite bewildered, because it must necessarily take this extra suggestion on trust.

Try to grasp that the fourth dimension is only really an extension of outlook.

Your eye is trained to be quite mentally aware of A, B. and C, though it is only really able to draw A and B ; the C is something in perspective. Now, having grasped that, your brain has only to go a single step further and it will grasp that when you try to express throughness in space, it is really not such a long step as it seems.

When once past the general grasp of the cosmic numbers, one, two, and three (which, after all, can be understood simply as the numbers indicating the first law of being, becoming and of maintaining all the diverse forms brought into being by the union of the first and second numbers), FOUR attempts to gain access to the world or state invisible.

THREE made life intelligible to the human mentality, but FOUR makes that which is invisible, intangible, abstract, incomprehensible, unknown, and so far unknowable in the concrete, attainable as a very real experience.

Your mind may be quite able to believe all these postulates about God's creations, various planes, different grades of evolutions not now known to man's ordinary senses, but when it tries to touch the fourth dimension, then it is going to find out the actual truth of all these suppositions, hypotheses, and so forth, for then your own knowledge of spiritual verities will be considerably enlarged and your own powers considerably enhanced.

Now let us try to convince your readers of the very real necessity for the broadening-out of their own consciousness, if they are to make proper soul progress. Too long the Christian churches have been the centres of knowledge fit for the kindergarten of life ; when all these centuries the civilization has been growing up, going into higher school classes (to pursue this metaphor), the religious teaching has stood still, and so nowadays your mentality from the religious point of view is infantile, though life is nearly at the end of its adolescent period.

In the old days when men and women had arrived at certain stages in their mental devolopment, they began to direct their attention to learning the higher development of their mentalities. They sought to learn through occultism, or, by training their intuitions, to make contact with a higher and fuller understanding of God and His creation, and how it all affected their own pathway towards the goal : for remember, no class of religious understanding has ever wavered in its firm belief that the soul was only temporary tenant of the present-day environment. The soul was always the one thing permanent to all sufficiently advanced in thought, in education, and in family traditions. That is why there is always a belief in the after-life in all religions. Your mind cannot conceive life on this very limited earth-plane as apart from the real life somewhere in infinity or in a wider sphere of some kind or other. Human intelligence smiles at anything so trivial as belief in one life here, and then a perpetual sleep, or, as your own church foolishly teaches, perpetual singing and rejoicing that your sins have been sponged away in a heaven of pearly gates and golden streets.

There is a very blessed state to which all are taken for a spell to rest and refresh their weary souls, but it is no more permanent than is your life on earth, for the soul is really a very complex and wonderful organism, and its development takes aeons of time and many planes of varied experiences.

So many folk come over here full of stupid ideas and are disappointed and very difficult to manage ; we wish more real spiritual knowledge was given, and then progress in your own sad world would work out at a much speedier rate of proper and wise development.

The days will come when disease will not kill, and when death itself, as your folk now understand it, will not mean all the horror which now surrounds its outward severance of man's bodies, but a gentle parting of atomic coverings, bringing no real sense of desolation to those left behind, and much enjoyment and not loneliness to those who make the journey over here.

So, then, the number FOUR is the number of that which lies immediately beyond the ordinary sight of men, that is the fourth dimension. It is the number which gives much contact with forces usually connected with all that is unreachable to the everyday consciousness. Shall we give your minds a few very useful hints about this contact ?

Well, then, begin by imagining that your body is standing on the point of a very high mountain ; your eyes make no attempt to look down, for that would mean destruction, nor any attempt to look to the right or to the left for there is no foothold ; your mind cannot imagine how your body ever got there, but since it has, your mind knows it cannot stay there for ever, so it must make a move somewhere. The question is, where can it go without immediate death from falling? It can only go upwards on the wings of a dove or something equivalent. You cannot grow doves' wings to order, so your mind decides that if the ether is the only really solid thing in the universe, surely it can just shake off its bodily shape and flit away into a blue distance and all will be well.

If the ether is really solid and your body not solid at all, then it stands to reason your mind is going to see a new world of existence. We think if your minds would try this as a preliminary exercise, when your minds are quiet and your bodies safely deposited in your own homes, in case of sudden translation from your earth plane to this, your minds one day will make the voyage quite safely and happily; and then your hearts will be cured of all pettinesses, jealousies, doubts, and from all evil thoughts which at present assault and hurt your souls; and there will be no more death, for your minds will now realize that death is swallowed up in the light of reality.

Follow for a few moments another aspect of the number FOUR, which is most interesting and highly occult, for remember, numbers apply to the occult rather than to what is more spiritual or intuitional on the unseen planes.

Your mind is familiar with four seasons, four elemental kingdoms, four beasts of the apocalypse, four evangelists, four mental conditions of man's body (we mean, of course, the four temperaments): also four names of God in one, the four triangles on the square forming the pyramid, four sides of a square, four winds, four quarters of the globe, four banners: four is, in fact, a most prevalent number in connection with much that is well known on your earth plane. FOUR is the number used in building, as it gives the law of stability and of just proportion, and just as there must be proportion and stability in the building of stone edifices, so must there be due proportion and equilibrium in the building of the spiritual edifice of a man's character.

So in the measure of proportion the universe depends on the set form or number of four, and cosmic evolution has issued from the four kingdoms of elemental essences or elements. Your brain will see something fresh in the idea that there can be indeed sermons in stones, for all accurate and well-proportioned work in the erection of masonic structure is very much finer than your mind suspects.

Proportion, remember, is another form of truer rhythm, and the highest kind of spiritual life is the life spent in harmonious building of thought and of character in subtler matter, which some day makes an appearance in something of your own creation, a book, a poem, a picture, a man's dwelling place, a town planning, a vase, a garden : all these are more or less forms rhythmic or otherwise of God's gift to man of free and creative faculty.

Has your mind ever considered that there is always a special meaning in the different parts of your own bodies ? They correspond with certain principles in nature ; in fact, so closely is your whole being bound up with what your people term nature, that a very great truth is entailed in the idea that knowledge even of the truth of one small flower would furnish your own world with a radiance of creative knowledge quite unsuspected.

God deals with all classes of beings, with every plane of existence to make His scheme perfect ; all blend together in one great harmony of sound, sight, and colour ; and. only those who are prepared to see God in all things, even in the ugly and in the deficient, will at last find Him very close to their hearts. For God is a god of the infinite, whether small or great, evil or good, just or unjust ; all that your hearts deplore in everyday life must be helped, guided, loved, understood, and never condemned nor criticized unduly in any way, for all will ultimately find their own way home to Him.

What really matters is the speed with which this return can be speeded up as your minds call it.

FOUR, then, in conclusion, shows the soul's way to realization on the higher dimension of consciousness.

FIVE.

To-day we are going to write about the number FIVE, which is the special number of Initiation or the special advancement of the individual soul on its homeward journey.

When a man's soul is finding that the joys and sorrows of your earth life are very unsatisfactory and full of change in every method of expression, he naturally turns to find some one thing that is permanent in a world of shadows, illusions, and of outwardly changing forms.

Once more he is driven within his own being to find, as the mystics write, his own centre ; the centre round which he cannot lose his way or go astray. Your Masonic ritual explains this very lucidly ; your mind can follow all that we say very simply, for all must emanate from a centre placed somehow in the midst of a man's own exoteric and esoteric grasp of things.

Having found a centre which can never be false because it can never be falsified, it being that inherent divine spark hidden within a man's own soul, he next proceeds to make contact with other forces in the only way possible to him as a human being, that is, through his five senses.

Now these senses are very rightly typical of the greatest forces found in the great elemental kingdoms of this system of your own. They are the five gates of sensory knowledge, the five gates through which every sort of trial will walk in and overcome your soul, or the five barriers which your own soul may raise to keep off all intruders to your own holy of holies.

It is a very strange fact, but a very true one, that when a man once begins to understand that his soul is something more than a merely secondary part of his physical body, at once the physical body begins to assert itself in a very marked fashion ; it is explained by the ordinary occultists by saying that in stepping apart from his ordinary fellow-beings, the newly awakened man attracts to his own aura all the outpourings of strong magnetic forces, so that he begins by being greatly stirred up until all the dross or scum, or whatever your mind may choose to call it, is cleared away.

In a measure this is very true, but it goes much deeper than this, for when a man stands apart from his fellows to start his own homeward journey, he draws into his aura certain of the responsibilities of the sins of the whole world. Now do you see, your mind may catch at the fringe of a very deep mystery that lies at the back of all the ideas of vicarious atonement ; he is not a scapegoat, but as one who seeks to be admitted into the old partnership with his God and Heavenly Father ; he is also expected to assume part of the responsibilities of that partnership. To simplify this idea you might also say he is making a very wise business proposition, and whilst he gains the advantage of this divine partnership, he must shoulder his portion of the debts and credits of its outward seeming. Now you can see that whilst all must pay their own just debts for themselves, the newly joined partner must do all in his power to help, guide, and safeguard his newly made responsibility.

That is the reason that FIVE is the number of the initiate, the number of the elder brother, the number of the saviour. It is the number of sudden summing up of life's responsibilities ; it is the number of clairvoyance, of clairaudience, of clairsentience, of clairolifactoriness, and of intuitional discrimination.[1]

The five senses, as your own physical body knows them, are of course only physical expressions of what is much finer and of those powers which are extended as soon as the soul awakens to its responsibilities, to its own line of evolution. The first three are well understood already by all intelligent beings, but the next two require a further explanation.

The sense of smell on your earth plane is not so important as the others, because your people regard it as something peculiar to savages and animals. Your mind thinks only of pleasing and unpleasing smells ; you are attracted by the sense of perfect beauty in the perfumes of flowers and repelled by the odour of dirt and decay and all evil things ; but as a matter of fact, smell is a very much more subtle sense than these two parts of it. Not only do we learn here to sense a man's development through his appearance, that is through his sound, colour, and form, but he has his own odour, too, a very subtle form of vibration ; it is a highly spiritual one, too, connected with the wonderful idea of the great Breath of Life imparted at the beginning by the great Creator when He is said to have breathed into Man the breath which made him a living soul.

You must begin to understand now at last the very wonderful connection there is between a man's body and

---

[1] Do you mean discrimination ? Yes, your mind cannot receive the exact word because what we actually mean is not a word in your own language, but your brain follows the drift of our meaning and that is the main thing after all.

the powers of the Great Oversoul, and in time your mind will grasp what is really behind diseases.[1]

We have to consider the significance of the number FIVE from another point of view, that of the larger idea of what is cosmic in outlook. There is a point when that which is purely human is placed in juxtaposition with what is purely divine, and Man, in the experience known to him as his spiritual resurrection, is lifted up before all eyes.

Now here is a very profound mystery. The soul in its spiritual birth was symbolized by the five-pointed star seen by the wise men, who of course are only symbols of the states of the soul's progress in a great mystery drama ; but now in this later state you have the wonderful mystery picture of the raising aloft of the completely developed soul, a figure on a cross, a figure with wounded head, hands, and feet, pierced at the centre. Your religious feeling for what is mystical can picture the beauty and the marvel of this idea, for as the perfect Man is raised up for all to love and understand, even so must each individual man through initiation (which is only another term for definite soul progress) be raised in turn to be an encouragement and an example for humanity. Now you can so much better understand the necessity for reintroducing the Christian mysteries.

SIX.

SIX is the number of balance. Its symbol is the union of the two triangles, known as the interlaced triangles or Solomon's Seal. It is connected with the centre and foreshadows the number seven. All is balanced from the centre and these two triangles are typical of the macrocosm and the microcosm, or God as King of Heaven and Man as King of Earth.

You see Man has gone a step higher, he is a King, a Ruler, not just the Perfect Man or Initiate. Just as the first three principles meant Being, Becoming, and Maintaining in the Cosmos, and were all worked out from God the One, so in this second trinity you have the being, becoming, and maintaining of Man in the lower Cosmos. Man, as it were, does maintain the world, he runs it, it is his special place.

[1] See *Healing*, p. 150.

FOUR gives the elemental kingdoms forming the world ; FIVE gives man's duty as saviour of the world ; and SIX gives his position as ruler ; so here your mind sees again the truth of the axiom, " as above, so below."

SIX is the number of Love, or, as the Greeks called her, Venus ; and Venus is, as your mind knows, the planet of Libra, the scales of balance.[1]

Now Love has a very special significance at this point, for Love, in its perfection, must possess full knowledge or it is worthless. It is the real touchstone of all that sums up the history, spiritual, moral, and physical, of the whole universe. Can you not see that only when your hearts understand this wonderful truth can you judge, help, rule, teach ?

Put out of your mind any idea of passion. Love is highest wisdom, strictest justice, greatest sacrifice ; nothing less, nothing human at this stage, but something too great to be put into your feeble language.

The most wonderful thing in your earth life is love, because it is the truest expression of what God is, carried from on high into your own physical plane. The more your heart expands in a widening out of the love nature, rather than concentration on man's own special family alone, the more wonderfully evolved will the evolution of the soul become. Make loving service one of the objects of your life, and what will happen to others a matter of real import- ance to your own self, and your heart shall more closely understand what is meant by the Fatherhood of God ; for this expression of Fatherhood is not an idle tale, it is a great cosmic fact and man's very composition as potential father or mother is a bond of the greatest importance and significance. Your desire to render service to others is a definite measure of your own spiritual progress.

" Who are my father and mother ? " said your great example, Christ. He knew the great importance of love on the highest and widest scale. That is why all mankind must learn to love much more than at present is the general rule.

Love is the fulfilling of the law of the Cosmos, the law of the Universe, the law of great planetary beings, the law of

[1] Astrologically six is given as the number of Venus, and Venus is the ruler of the sign Libra.

c

human progress; and only by love may man approach within the Holy of Holies.

Now when your mind has grasped the inner meaning of Love Divine, Cosmic, and All-pervading, turn for a moment in spirit to the very great teaching of the ancient Egyptians, who conceived of the number SIX as the great seal of wisdom, hence it was called Solomon's Seal by a later dispensation, for the six-pointed star is, as your mind is fully aware, another name for the six Points of Wisdom, namely, the point of love, the point of sympathy, the point of joy, the point of faith, the point of unity, the point of harmony.

CORRESPONDENCES.

Our own understanding of the great cosmic marks in the outer worlds is not on the lines at all of what your people call correspondences, for the true mark of correspondence is not on the earth plane at all, it is in the Heaven world where all counterparts exist. The idea is not known that as a general rule that which your own eye sees is not the true thing but its shadow. Your eye sees all through a glass darkly and not face to face.

Do you not sense how very wise all this is, for by sensing the truth inwardly your soul grows toward the true light, while the shadows which your perishing body senses must of necessity perish, too, for otherwise your five senses would not sense them at all; all is illusion in one sense, because all which your physical body considers real is no more real than your physical body is real. It is not reality in essence, it is only reality in a very small degree, and not the important essence as your mind thinks.

We are always amazed to find your body is so sensitive to outward suffering, because it is so much a matter of illusory shadow and not permanent in any measure; but we are quite aware that your very sensitiveness is part of your own usefulness to the great spirits, as the more sensitive your soul is to the sickness and sorrow of the world, the more will your love of sufferers increase and that will bring about a very much better state of affairs in the outer world in general.

That which your heart deplores, that which antagonizes

your mind, that which arouses the real pitiful love of your spirit is that divine thing which will cleanse, purify, and exalt the human being into a higher state of realization of its own partnership with godliness and all the wonderful attributes of divinity. Cultivate this love spirit.

We, who watch the struggles of mankind towards some blind goal, which the religious-minded call Heaven, and the ethical-minded call the Millennium, we often long to show the way through the darkness ; not from our side but from your own world must rise the Light that lighteth every man, for all search after Truth must be free and undivided in effort.

We watch always for such as love to serve, they are all saviours of their own kind and of them it has been said " of such is the Kingdom of Heaven," for their love will open up paths to their great and marvellous God, Whose Being is always in evidence in the meanest of His creatures.

Never despair of human beings, they are all working out their own line of salvation, but do all you can to encourage, praise, and stimulate the feeble glimmer which resides in the soul of all things. Now think on all this, and when your soul grows weary and ill with the apparent failure, know that at least there are those who watch all your efforts and who in time will show your blindness the first glimpse of a dawning splendour.

Take no thought for the morrow, the promise of the future is in the hands of your Heavenly Father. He shall accomplish all things in the fulness of time, for all things are hastening towards the goal of perfection. Let your mind rise to greater heights of hopefulness and of courage. The end can only be what is promised, and that is perfection, a making up of all the unevennesses of life, a true balance of accounts before the next era of civilization when this one is past. Nothing recedes to its past level, that is what your feeble understandings are apt to forget ; your new life era will start from a higher or quicker level ; and though time passes (in your own understanding of the word time), yet always the wheel of life spins at a higher and quicker rate of development, and things never go back to the same level, though the newly dispersed energy or soul-wave has to undergo the period of its childhood with all childhood's complaints and crudities ; all through the adolescent state of development to perfect manhood. All progresses, in spite of the appalling waste of material in time and other essential things.

They, whose lives on the earth plane finish with any special epoch or civilization, go on to other planes and continue in work more suited to them; they have finished their course, they receive new outer bodies and go on somewhere else, leaving the earth plane for those whose experience is as yet incomplete.

CHAPTER III

THE SPIRITUAL SIGNIFICANCE OF NUMBERS (*contd.*)

SEVEN. The Number of Complete Development. Seven a spiritual number. The Link between God and Man. Night and Morning. Seven used in invocation.
EIGHT. The Higher Degree of Consciousness.
NINE. The Three Trinities.
TEN. The number of the Great Father-Creator. The I AM. Spiritual Longing. Perfect Man and Perfect God. The Double Five. The Great Scientist, God. The Centre and the Circle.

SEVEN.

SEVEN is a very significant number, for it is the basic number of the mind of the earth, also the number of man's own full development on the material planes.

There are the seven planets, the seven senses, the seven rays of development, the seven notes of the scale, the seven years of famine, the seven years of plenty, the seven man's orifices known to the occultist as the seven chakras, in fact your pencil could go on indefinitely with this figure ; much is made clear to the soul that can sense the hidden mystery of SEVEN.

Your mind is aware of the mystical idea that the world was made in seven days. This is of course an allegory and has nothing to do with time, for of course the real idea of SEVEN with regard to human time seems very wrong to us and very difficult to make clear to your own mentality.

The fundamental teaching of SEVEN is not on the mental plane at all, but on the spiritual plane, which makes it more difficult to make clear to the consciousness of an ordinary human being ; but remember that it is a combination of the FOUR and the THREE, that is, it is the union of the cosmic trinity with the great mystery of the fourth dimension, which is the dimension of the first degree

37

outside the comprehension of the microcosmic trinity of man.

Now your brain has caught a glimpse of this mystery, Perfect God, Perfect Man and the link connecting them. SEVEN is indicative of all that is perfect, two trinities held together at the centre which is Reality. Your finite minds do not understand the significance of Reality, the great cosmic essence which permeates all things which endure, and of whom it was written " sorrow endureth for a night yet joy cometh in the morning." Night and morning are here used on the great and mystical scale of light (that is, mental and spiritual light) ; and whilst morning is, of course, the symbol of dawn, of light ; sorrow or night means the period employed by the mind and spirit in incarnation in gross heavy particles of materialism.

Whenever this number SEVEN is used it denotes more than a mere counting up of a material number of days or years, it means the connecting link in point of time between your world and ours.[1]

The number SEVEN is very occult and also very powerful ; it may be very dangerous too if wrongly invoked as it rouses strange forces in the elemental kingdoms.

Whenever your mind is making any use of numbers for the purpose of contacting unseen things, your own power would be increased if your invocation were used seven times ; as, for example, if your mind were set on making contact with someone at a distance for healing, or for the purposes of influencing them in any way, if your tongue uttered their names seven times it would become a powerful mantram. Never put this knowledge to unlawful uses, it would harm yourself. Whenever your own selfish ends are considered then all occult knowledge becomes very dangerous.

EIGHT.

The number EIGHT is, as your mind is aware, the usual number of constructive masonry, for it is the number used to give some definite form or plan of a very mystical and occult building.

[1] Time seems to indicate somehow a condition of space.—M.B.

The EIGHT, which is a double cube, is, of course, typical of material on two planes of substance, and as such it may be used to imply that which is more solid from the point of view of your own world, but we regard this number rather from another point of view.

It is very difficult to bring certain ideas into the language of your own earth planet, for it is very limited, and what we know ourselves is very often quite outside any language by which we could convey to your mind what is very simple to us on these inner planes.

Now when we write of what is limited to the fourth dimension it is already too difficult to tell your brain what this fourth dimension is, how much more so when the number EIGHT is a full extension of that already incomprehensible dimension. It is FOUR carried to a higher degree of consciousness; it is really the state of mind which no human idea can fathom, the actual dimension or special idea of the spiritual building, a cosmic conception of all creative principles, to understand which would give to the human mind the true gift of being able to create life. That is why your wise men fail so much, they seek such knowledge from without, it must of necessity be within, and we use this word " within " ill-advisedly, for your language has no word to convey the actual position of invisible forces at all.

Nothing is within or without, all exists, and your scientists can only glimpse what is on the surface after much labour, and never what is all through, all pervading or penetrating, until they begin, as indeed a very few are already doing, to look outside or away from those facts which they note so very carefully in their own laboratories.

NINE.

The number NINE is the number which gives the three trinities on the three planes of matter, which your people call body, soul, and spirit, but which we call the three planes of manifestation, for manifestation is very clearly indicated on all three. We must tell your readers that these many members are, of course, only to be regarded as symbols of the principles involved.

Let us suppose for instance that the first triangle stands

for the great trinity of what we will call, for convenience, the Godhead ; then, of course, the second, which shows Man as the reflection of this cosmic trinity, and then we have this third trinity standing for the Universe. Now the Universe is the most material of all three trinities because it has no special gift of control of itself nor of mankind. Blind force is the ruler here to all appearances, but in reality the laws are strictly followed and there is no blindness at all, only a foolish idea made vocal by man's stupidity.

This third trinity is ruled by other beings of whom your own people are mostly unconscious.[1]

This third triangle completes the proper numbers, all others are amplifications of these various numbers.

The Oversoul of the Universe which composes this third triangle is full of immense powers not to be handled lightly in any way.

There are four elemental kingdoms, as your mind knows, but these kingdoms all belong to the most wonderful Order of Beings, quite apart from your own people and also apart from us here. They work with the great Cosmic Essence, who is wrongly called God, your Heavenly Father ; but this Cosmic Essence is not in actual fact your own God at all, for the First Great Cause is not your God, who is more closely linked up with your own selves in every way. These great Cosmic Beings are part of the immeasurable scheme of universe-creations and exist in an analogous triple state corresponding to body, soul, and spirit. It is all too vast to imagine or speak about. Do not try to comprehend too much, this knowledge is staggering to anyone in the material man's body.

TEN.

Now let us try to tell you about this very wonderful vibration known to your world as the mystery of the One containing All in its greatest and fullest conception ; for as we have said so often, numbers are very full of spiritual mysteries, which may be touched when the disciple is ready for much fuller development of knowledge. When this is accomplished the power to teach and to understand will be very greatly increased, and your vibrations rendered

[1] See *Devas*, p. 59.

much more sensitive to sights and sounds, hitherto unsensed by your mind. The wind is full of sounds which the ordinary ear misses ; yet your own wireless receives them. Your ears may be even more sensitive than these machine-made contrivances, if your own denser material faculties were purified and sufficiently refined. The sun will display colours, many of which are quite unknown to your own world, much more beautiful, much more rarefied.

This number TEN is really the number of the Great Father and Creator of all things, whom, quite erroneously, your people call God ; for indeed, He is unnamable, and unimaginable, and unknowable, for He is the great I AM, the All-in-All, the Great Cosmic Consciousness, the Over-soul, the Mind Discarnate and Incarnate, the Point in the Circle, the All-seeing, never-closed Eye.

This very great teaching is the essence of Royal Arch teaching, and of all mystery teachings. This is the real necessity for the schools of mystery teaching ; by winding spirals, by angles, triangles, squares, and such symbols is Man led up to the point within the circle, which is the perfection of knowledge, the knowledge of what is behind all manifestation.

Know then, that he who would know God must of necessity withdraw from the hurry of material life and listen to Him in the hurricane, in the raging of the sea, in the cry of humanity, in the innumerable sounds all about him, for there God is ; only He must be singled out in the silence of celestial sounds, in silence of the soul's ecstasy, in the great spiritual moments of the heart's devotion.

Like as the hart desireth the water-brooks, so let your purified heart long for God. This spiritual longing will ever remain unsatisfied by the vital experiences of life's turmoil. By sadness, loneliness, trials, tests, and by joys unspeakable also (for joy may be a test as well as sorrow), will the soul find its resting-place in the bosom of the Almighty God essence.

These ineffable mysteries must be sought for diligently, they never come to a man unbidden, unstriven-for, or unwanted. Never try to make people follow, they must all be free to arise, free to search for themselves, free to desire God ; never urge, coerce, or otherwise inflict your

views on others ; if they need your help give it according
to the light that is within your heart ; your own experience
will be a torch to guide others to ask your advice or help.
Never let anyone seek to deride your own ideas, never
argue, nor make yourself aggressive. Cast no pearls before
the unheeding, they must find these jewels themselves,
but writings help in an entirely different way ; they often
light the spark that ultimately shall illumine the whole of
the life into pleasant havens and quiet places of the soul.
This symbol of TEN is very occult, as well as highly
spiritual. It will make double FIVE, and thus shows Perfect
Man and Perfect God. It is really the number of crucifixion, for crucifixion is an experience of Higher Consciousness, and not of material death at all : spirit within matter,
matter exalted into purest spiritual altitudes.

Now when this state is fully understood as an experience
spiritual and not a physical fact, then Christianity will be
set up on high as the greatest revelation of all ages. But
the idea of death must not remain, for death is not important
at all, it is negligible, a mere passing experience of the
pilgrim soul, an experience often repeated until it has
assumed its proper place in the consciousness of the ordinary
man's mind. This will show itself more and more in the
newer teaching as time evolves the intelligence of human
minds along these lines of understanding. That is what we
wish this book specially to teach.

It will not be a book for the ignorant and unintelligent,
for the ignorant are not ready for higher knowledge ; their
time will be later in their own experiences. But this teaching will help many whose hearts seek diligently for the Light
that lighteth every man in his innermost soul.

These signs, tokens, symbols, or numbers really carry,
hidden for the wise, secrets of natural forces in creation ;
such forces may or may not be revealed, that depends on
the seeker, and maybe the reader will see the hidden suggestion and awake to this greater unfoldment of God's
Wisdom, Strength, and Beauty.

All life is built up on symbols emanating from the unseen
laboratory of the Great Scientist, God. Why do your
people quarrel about the difference between religion and
science ? They are only aspects of one united manifestation
or creation ; for Creation is like a wonderful diamond many-

faceted, and God's celestial beauty radiates from out each facet with equal splendour.   Bow your heads in reverential love before all these facets of creation ; your foolish limitations are only set by your ignorance.   God sets no limits at all.

Seek and ye shall find Him everywhere.   Knock and He shall open all gateways into His own sanctuaries to the worthy and pure in heart.   Rest assured of the great bracing power of the Circle which is the aura of God, and within it no man may be lonely or cut off from life eternal.

CHAPTER IV

NATURE FORCES

(a) *The Soul of the Universe*

The Group-soul. The Oversoul. The Astral plane of animals. Nature's Destiny. Nature's Tooth and Claw. Killing for Food. Occult Science. Nature Forces. Magic. Nature the Great Mother. Cosmos and Chaos. Perpetual Motion. Vibrations.

THE Soul of the Universe is a cosmic subject, and requires very good conditions, because there are points in it which touch undreamed-of heights, and when these matters are to be sent into the ordinary minds of men, we have to make the vibrations very attenuated and very finely tuned in, or the ideas will not impinge correctly on our human medium's consciousness.

Know then, that the soul of the universe is of much greater extent than the mind of man can grasp in the most shadowy method of thought.

This soul differs from the soul of man's evolution, because the soul of man has within it certain faculties of the God Who is the Heavenly Father of Mankind, and in this picture of God as a Father, man is able to measure his own potentialities, for just as man was made in the image of his Father-God, so he inherits those faculties which a son inherits from his father, although in a very small and remote degree.

Within the soul of the universe all beings have their existence, but their individuality is very different, for there is much more the idea of group-souls, as was taught in the Eastern methods of wisdom teaching. Their mistake lay in the fact that they presumed the group-soul crystallized into a human soul later in evolution, but such was not the case, the lines of evolution are entirely different.

Now, the group-soul is entirely dependent on the great

Oversoul of their own line of evolution ; there is no free will at all. In man's evolution, though his soul is a spark struck off from the mass OVER-SOUL, yet each single spark is *free* to become a divine being in due course, or *free* to be annihilated if it should so desire.

The goal of the group-soul is purely to exist as a group ; there is no individualized goal. When the physical sheath of these creatures perishes, or becomes disintegrated, the group-soul gathers the soul part, and uses it again for the same kind of evolution. The group-soul may be likened to a kind of pervading essence of life, which is poured into various physical forms, to be released and re-absorbed when the physical form ceases to exist. This does not apply to the warm-blooded animals ; their line of evolution is again quite different, and may be drawn by man into his own aura for good or evil. The goal of such creatures is always very uncertain to the human mind, for many learn to love these creatures, and as we have told you, love will draw them back again into the aura of their owners in other lives.

There is a world or sphere where animals, whose souls are more advanced, may live a kind of astral life happily enough, and some reincarnate very regularly into human families, but many merely enter into animal bodies indiscriminately until their final dissolution into another form of soul essence.

Now when the soul of the universe is to be used for new forms of life it is recalled into the hidden spheres and is re-issued under new forms for new life on other planes, not necessarily physical earth planes, for universal soul is spread out into myriads of forms unknown to your own earth planet.

This is very important to remember when it occurs to the human mind to bewail the waste and cruelty of nature. Nature goes on her own pilgrimage without heeding man, for she must fulfil her own destiny, just as man must fulfil his. If his body is caught in Nature's cataclysms, it is neither the cruelty of nature nor the injustice of the Heavenly Father which should be blamed, but man's own self-chosen destiny, which has placed his little body in that predicament in order that his greater soul may acquire that special experience.

Nothing is purposeless. All moves in a finely planned

design and man's highest good must be to realize this perfection of design behind all the sorrows and joys of mortal life.

Life is only mortal in one tiny aspect, for Life is a grand plan of wondrous change, and marvellous arrangement of each petty detail from the life of a cell to the life of an entire solar system.

"BE STILL AND KNOW THAT I AM GOD." These are words of wonderful comfort, for the Great Designer, the Wondrous Architect, will never blunder, nor miscalculate any part of His stupendous task.

The Kingdom of Nature is vast. It has its own special ministers, its own laws, its own penalties and rewards.

Your heart is upset by Nature's tooth and claw, yet the suffering in Nature's realm, where there is not a very highly developed nervous organization, is not one-tenth as terrible as the suffering imposed by sentient, so-called "loving" man on his own kind, not to speak of the suffering inflicted by him on the lower forms of life.

Your mind revolts against Nature's apparent heedlessness. Your mind sees only the ugly side of destruction, yet Nature has this mercy—remember, there is no real pre-knowledge of death ; there is no real knowledge of loss by death— there is a speedy oblivion. Anticipation has no place amongst the wild creatures. Man teaches fear ; he tortures in traps, he experiments, he enslaves ; he teaches animal creation to love, dread, and hate. That is when real suffering enters into animal life.

It is quite impossible to tell all that exists in the way of compensating laws in the realm of Nature. It is all perfectly adjusted and each is given its own line of defence. Let us tell you this for your own satisfaction—the man who refuses to be led into trapping, killing, for sport or for food, is a long way on the path of living in tune with the infinite wonders of the Kingdom of Nature. Food is, of course, too great a problem at this stage to be entirely reconstituted ; we can only suggest the giving up of real animal food, as speedily as is compatible with health, by all those who start on this great pilgrimage of spiritual evolution.

Your doctors are already beginning to talk about a no-meat diet, and we watch their efforts with keenest interest. Fruit is the natural food of man with cereals, but only comparatively few maintain their proper standard of health on this limited diet. In the dim future food will have entirely altered ; meanwhile become pioneers as far as possible.

There is, of course, a scientific (so-called) side of the Nature Forces, and these are such forces as the real understanding of the laws of gravity, of attraction and of repulsion, of rays, of cells, and of all the infinitesimal forms of life established by science, yet not visible to the ordinary eye or mind, that is, to the brain. These laws are understood by the occultist, and as time passes occultists will become the acknowledged scientists of your world, and this will be when the fourth dimension is a commonly accepted dimension. Your people will have gone one step further in their mental evolution, and the rest will follow.

We will now give your mind some points on the subject of Nature forces.

As you are already aware, there are many strange influences quite unsuspected by the usual man or woman, forces which are occult, and are strangely linked up with the great natural forces which render increase of life (in a physical sense) powerful and possible on your earth planet. Your mind asks if they are evil ? They are not evil in the cosmic sense of the word, but they are not the spiritual side of the soul's evolution, and while they may be understood and studied, there should be a very distinct barrier raised between the soul of Man stretching out toward perfection, and this curious soul-essence of Nature in these half-human forms, for the human soul is of the real divine origin, but the nature soul is of a very different vibration.

The line of demarcation is reached in every revelation of divine wisdom ; that is really where the danger lies for the soul which has advanced up to a certain point ; and this is the point at which the white magic declares itself as something apart from the so-called black magic. Remember, we use this word magic in its real meaning, that which is wisdom of the original kind ; not knowledge which is acquired wisdom, but original or fundamental wisdom.

Occultism is really the science of this hidden wisdom, and where it is used for unlawful purposes it becomes evil ; but used merely for the purpose of stimulating the hidden vibratory centres of Man's being, for signs, words, or gesture, rhythmic movements, breathing, or chants, then the senses are of the highest value, but the motive must always be for the adoration of the Great Being, who made all these powerful forces, and in order to bring the human entity into a closer and more understanding vibration with HIM who is the great author or progenitor of all human creation ; that Divine Being who once walked and talked with the soul of Man in the days of his primordial beauty and righteousness.

This many-sided being, which your minds call Nature, cosmic, relentless, all-pervading, omnipresent (yet neither omniscient nor omnipotent, for that is alone GOD), this Nature, as your minds call this vast Mother of material manifestation, is, in her own way, a very great Divine Body also, since she supplies the fecund womb and the material for all those creatures inspired, created, or projected from out of His own Over-mind, the Father-God ; she is the divine spouse, the ever-youthful bride, the desire of the Absolute, the Second person of the Cosmic Trinity.

Now turn for a moment towards the other aspect of this Mother Nature, for she is the Mother of all living beings, of all that is manifest, and even unmanifest, in the ordinary ways of your earthly life and consciousness. This bounteous Mother, this Divine Being, who is too vast to be realized, even as the Absolute Being is too vast to be imagined, this Nature is permeated with a wonderful beauty, a vast love, which is the reason for existence ; this is the true meaning of existence and of sex-union ; for Love, Cosmic and All-pervading, is the ruling force of the DIVINE FATHER-MOTHER-GOD, and all of us, yourselves, ourselves, and all the myriad forms and varieties of natural manifestation, are the children of that amazing Cosmic Union.

Can your intellect not see that the Union of Cosmos, the male or inspirational Element, with Chaos, the female or receptive Element, has resulted in a stupendous and unrealizable force, which we can only term Universal Discrimination ; and that this force of discrimination has resulted in the splitting up into complete and independent forms of evolved beings, each following its special wave of vibration, which quivers in the inchoate matrix of indistinguishable essences of forms in a state of flux.

This dynamic force must forever vibrate throughout all time, space, and throughout all forms of living beings ; that is the secret of perpetual motion, that is why vibration is the real mainspring of all forms of being. Vibration is the expulsion of the Absolute, energizing in form, or manifestation, and when the mind of Man really begins to grasp the barest fringe of this idea, he will begin to understand something of his own link with the limitless ; in spite of limitations he will begin to understand how the less contains the greater, and how there is neither great nor small, for all is a stupendous and never beginning nor ending stream of perfect and divine existence, expressed by motion or energy.

Vibration will in time be realized as the actual source and expression of existence in all planes of matter, and in this meaning of the word " matter " we would imply being of all description. Matter is, of course, most unsuited as a term of expression, for matter presupposes, in your own terms of speech, a collection of cells worked up into a more or less dense mass or substance, but really matter is full of space and only held by the will of the spirit in another plane of existence, for, of course, matter makes contact everywhere with spirit there is nothing without spirit. Much exists only in spirit ; the real limits are the few varieties of forms in matter, which may seem very strange to your minds, which are very much impressed with the many forms of matter ; your eyes see such a myriad of forms, yet the myriads unseen by your physical eyes would defy all possible form of description. Now when these first signs of manifested life began to be seen on your earth, your own spiritual bodies were yet unveiled, but were immanent in the womb or matrix of the spiritual force known as the Oversoul, the Divine Mother, the Virgin. Think how much wider your conception of the universe must become if your puny brains begin to see that all existence is of one divine source, for that will begin to remove the amazing conceit of the ignorant, who often regard God as a Being set up to minister to their puny desires for ephemeral well-being. Let this idea be freely spread abroad, that GOD is the Absolute, is the Unrealizable of man's mind ; that God the Heavenly Father is the great and wonderful Being in charge of man's own special development ; that Man is by the universal

D

law of existence divine, and possessed of divine powers in a greater or lesser degree, as he himself shall will, and that Jesus the Christ is Man's own King of all Glory, and of Life Eternal, the most completed spiritual form of God the Heavenly Father.

So is Man's place in the universe distinct, and most necessary to the general plan of the Great Absolute I AM. For even as the smallest point in a vast machine is as necessary to the general working of that machine, so is Man the microcosm, the miniature god in the germ (as it were), necessary to the great and stupendous whole as planned out in the mind of GOD.

VIBRATIONS.

Q. Can you tell us what vibrations are ? Do you mean oscillations as our scientists do ? Are *higher* vibrations quicker vibrations ?

A. This is a most difficult question to answer. Vibration is the beginning of existence, as we have already told you. Oscillation is the very elementary type of vibration which has become a commonplace to your minds through your ideas of wireless ; they are a very faint copy of the real cosmic vibrations.

Vibrations are the pulse of the Great I AM. Vibration is the great cosmic force of divine, energizing, perpetual motion.

That is perfectly clear, but when your human minds try to put this cosmic idea into language, your minds are stopped, because what is cosmic is difficult to put into your language. This idea of vibration, as known to your scientists, is something of the same nature, the earth-plane counterpart of a cosmic force ; but one day your earth-plane people will know much more, and your minds will see that one is the very feeble copy of the great original force.

CHAPTER V

(*b*) *Creation of Form*

Flowers. Music of the Universe. Nature's Deities. Devas. Man's influence on Nature.

EARTH is full of a great variety of forms, God fulfils Himself in many ways of beauty, that is why the idea about the immanence of God in all life exists in your minds.

Try to understand what is meant by form. It is the collecting of ideas from other planes, that is, ideas from the Creator Himself, and putting them into vehicles of coarser matter to convey a veritable truth to the world in general.

Do you not see that any distortion in the mind of the medium would mean ugliness, abortion, in fact sin itself ? Sin is really an abortion of man's mind quite as much as a lack of development of his mental faculties ; so you can see that it was very important that those who taught the outside world should be pure and undefiled, and only anxious to permeate the world with the real knowledge of Beauty that is God made manifest. Simplicity in design is the highest form of truth—when the tortuous mind of man begins to amplify it, then truth is in danger of becoming a very bewildering thing and men are led astray like sheep. When men strain after effect, they lose sight of the real fundamental principles of God and become entangled in a network of unnecessary, outside, petty things, which finally lead to misconceptions of Him and of the highest and best and simplest of teachings.

It is a fact that every form in your material world has its counterpart in the higher realms of the soul planes.

All design is, as your mind understands, a symbol of ideas

in existence on the higher mental planes ; the Mind of God is full of all these varying manifestations in Nature's kingdom.

You wonder why flowers exist—is it to be just a joy given to the human race ? Because they do bring much happiness into your earth plane. That is, however, not the reason for their creation ; it is a very wonderful reason really ; it is this—that the vibrations of all floral life are very finely tuned-in to catch the expression of certain tones of the Great Song of the Universe.

The universe is planned on a musical scale, with many tones, far more numerous than any human musician can possibly understand. All life fulfils some portion of that music just as in a great orchestra the completed harmony is rendered possible by the blending of many instruments, and the score is composed of various signs which render the reading of that score intelligible to the conductor, who is there to interpret the great design behind, which emanated from the composer's brain.

It is difficult to imagine, perhaps, but all creation takes a definite part in the orchestra of the ALL-PERVADING-GOD, Whose designs are far beyond the understanding of even the more advanced spirits of our own higher sphere. We see more of the score than the humbler performers perhaps, but oh ! so little more ! and we are filled with the wonderful beauty and completeness of that score ; we can only praise, bless and magnify Him for ever and ever.

The smallest flower bears the stamp of this ALL-PERVADING-ONE. If more were understood of the law of signatures, more would be understood of His methods of writing in the secret pages of Nature.

There is actually a language of Flowers, the language which used to be understood by the simple country people, and which has become debased like many other languages.

All sounds of the growing of plant life are beautifully rhythmic, and, of course, all who feel this rhythm are of the elect of those who can tune-in with those fine vibrations, and Nature will always bring peace to their hearts in all times of stress and weariness.

Q. Are the great Devas conscious of human beings ?

A. Yes, that is the reason that the ancient wisdom is full of so-called Nature Deities, such as Pan, Orpheus, Demeter, Persephone, and others, all beautiful and in a

sense true Beings, for these embody the presiding Beings
in charge of the various branches of Nature's manifestations.
There are, to this day, certain among your own people
who quite consciously come into contact with these Deities,
or rather with these great Devas ; and they bear certain
unmistakable signs on their person. We know these signs,
but they are not always recognized by other human
beings.

They have strange powers over all wild things. They
are natural healers ; they are always wild, uncertain,
wayward people, free from diseases, and usually rather
feared by their fellow beings.

They are not quite on the usual line of evolution of
mankind, but are a type by themselves ; it is only a question
of soul development really ; the goal is the same, yet their
descent is really through older and more primitive races ;
they have outlived the physical race which originally gave
them embodiment, and they are a little strange in the
embodiment of the later races.

The Devas are entirely free of all human interference ;
they rule their own Kingdoms, and even though the civilization of a new race may, on the surface, appear to destroy
the stronghold of these Nature spirits, there are still realms
within realms untouched, and there is no real breaking
down of their influence.

They are not visible to any human eye, however developed
in clairvoyance. The Nature spirits are visible very often,
but not these great Devas ; they are formed of very different
vibrations, and having never been in human bodies, they
remain apart from human vision or hearing. They are not
astral by any means.

All creation exists by the pleasure of the ALL-PERVADING-
GOD, and human beings were not His first nor His last
consideration ; that is man's amazing conceit. But all
creation is important in the scheme, and all created things
have their own special part in this scheme. Man, by
intelligent, humble, and adoring co-operation with this
scheme, is allowed a special participation in this great design :
he may assist God, he is necessary to God. Make yourselves
invaluable to God, that is the ideal to be touched ; faithful
servants working for and with Him ; faithful over small
things, working to be rulers over many.

Now the soul counterpart of living bodies such as animals, birds, vegetation, and so forth, is very dependent on the co-operation of Man's own soul with the soul of the Universe ; for there is a kind of emanation from both the oversoul of Nature and the oversoul of Mankind, which intermingles and sets up a kind of elementary soul essence, from which these other creatures take their soul material. This is the reason that all manifestations of life are interdependent. From man's magnetic body there issues this curiously subtle emanation, which is of great use to all the lower, or lesser, or rather, the less individualized, forms of life around his aura.

Different types of mankind influence their own particular classes of other life ; some give off emanations of special benefit to warm-blooded animals, others to birds, others to reptiles, others to vegetation, flowers, fruits, others to stones and minerals ; there is a kind of magnetic sympathy.

Your astrologers speak of planetary influences, and give every man a special colour, herb, tree, stone, animal ; it is in a measure true ; they possess some such affinity, but the real cause of this vibrational affinity is the emanation given off by their own magnetic bodies, which helps to provide soul-essence, or magnetic power, to these particular creatures.

Now when these creatures feel this magnetic emanation from a certain human being they draw it into their own bodies, and that develops their evolution, and stimulates their own vibration, so that a real current of invisible life is set up and all manifested life is knit up together in a very wonderful way. This magnetism may be spent unwisely because of the ignorance of people in general ; for sometimes these creatures absorb more magnetism than they should and the person suffers depletion. This is realized by your people in the way of vegetation, but not always in the way of animals or stones.

Jewels are highly magnetic, which accounts for many of the curious legends attached to them ; very often they have the additional advantage of long existence in the same physical form.

You have already been told how certain human beings also act adversely on one another; we refer to the human mollusc, of whom you have personal knowledge.

Q. Yet birds and animals seem to flourish best away from human kind : it is natural for them to shun them ?

A. This is apparently the case, but your mind must remember that your self is only conscious of a fragment of soul, and that the entire universe is filled with emanations of myriads of souls, so that it is quite impossible for any human being to realize that their emanations reach out into space and affect the lives of many creatures on all planes of existence. There is no real division of substance of the spirit, that is what is so incomprehensible to anyone enclosed within the limits of one small human body ; just as it is impossible for your feeble brain to realize the myriad lives within your own one single human body.

Nay, be not depressed at the vastness of this divine scheme of creation, it is all so perfect, and when life in its present limitations is at an end, your soul will be filled with joy unspeakable in the seeing and comprehending of what lies in store for the soul in its new freedom.

LIFE.

Q. Can you define that which we call Life ?

A. Let us imagine for a moment a physical world full of inert forms of men, animals, birds, flowers, and of all those objects most familiar to your eyes. These forms, being inert, are, as you would say, lifeless—that is, they would be moulds without the necessary contents which would make them sentient living beings. It is quite a false analogy, because the very idea of any mould or form presupposes a moving entity, or energy, or vibration, which caused certain material atoms to cling together to form those moulds ; there never was really a particular moment without life as your minds term it.

Yet wrongly for the moment we will imagine lifeless forms, and then we will remember that moment spoken of as the Divine Breathing In, and we will at once know that life, all life, is that Divine Breathing In, that setting into motion certain forces of repulsion and attraction, of expulsion and of reception or conception ; of involution and evolution ; of inspiration and expiration ; and we will know that life has always existed, because life is the moving, energizing factor behind all form, and behind every possible thinkable idea of material cohesion. Is life the soul ? Yes. Is life the spirit ? Yes. Is life the body accretion of atoms ? Yes. Is life the nucleus of the atom ? Yes. Life is Being on any plane of existence ; that inimitable all-pervading IS-NESS which is universal on all planes of existence.

CHAPTER VI

NATURE FORCES (*contd.*)

(c) *Nature Spirits*

ONE of the first signs of a linking-up with Nature's own special spirit forces is the realising of the presence in your midst of fairies, or Nature spirits, as your mind knows of these very charming little folk, whose special work it is to work in harmony with the growing of flowers and the guarding of much of the insect life amongst your own haunts. Your world is really greatly used by these creatures as a trial place for their experiments.

When Nature spirits wish to make a new manifestation, they make a very strong form of a subtle material which is not really ether at all, but something you do not know at all yet ; and they make use of the material world as a kind of factory for the coarser material. Then they call the new shape into being by the sounds which they can use, and the new plant or animal is henceforward a structure of the visible world.

Now if human beings are friendly with these beings they allow themselves to be seen. Nature spirits are not very high in the scale of evolution, but they live very merry lives and make your world very beautiful whenever they get a chance. Much would be understood about them if your people believed in them instead of scoffing about their existence. They are of etheric matter only, very tenuous, but most easily seen if the eye tunes-in to this very easily acquired clairvoyance.

Let us for a moment understand this kind of sight ; it is not so easy to explain it, of course, but it may best be understood when we tell your mind that etheric sight is the sight which depends on the eyes being very sensitive

57

to the varying tints of colour. No so-called colour-blind person can see these Nature spirits, but an artist, with very, very sensitive sight which reacts to the most varying and delicate vibrations of colour, can with practice see these Nature spirits very soon.

The ordinary eye looks quickly at colour and gets a mass impression, but train your eyes to discern the innumerable shades of colour in one colour, and very soon the eye discriminates much that is little suspected in a single gleam of colour.

Now carry this discrimination into the very stillness of your garden, your heath, or any place which is free to Nature's working out her own special way, and your eye will see Nature's workpeople doing their work, as if your foot turned over an ant-heap and your eyes suddenly saw the busy city of your friend the ant at work.

When your eyes have learnt to discern fairies or Nature spirits, your ear will next learn to hear sounds which it has little understood before in the songs of birds, and in the hum of insects ; for Nature's orchestra is a very large one indeed, and not dumb, as your foolish folk call creatures not gifted with speech such as your own tongues utter. Speech means the uttering or making audible a certain rate of vibration, tuned-in to beat against the ear tympanum. Sound of any kind is in reality speech. Machines make speech ; all growing things which your eyes delight in have their own language for your deaf ears. Now when your eyes are tuned-in to this first form of etheric sight, and your ears tuned-in to this etheric sound, you can understand that your understanding of Nature forces will carry you much further until the greater forces of storm, wind, rain, and such-like are forces which your mind will understand, and you will know that the so-called solid human body can be in such harmonious understanding with these forces that it will be friendly towards them, and not full of fear of them. This is the reason that certain great ones of your own earth plane have been able to walk on the water, still tempests, remove obstacles.

Did not your own Master Jesus say your faith could remove mountains ? This was no idle boast or fairy tale. He only pictured the immense possibilities open to all those who really understood the great universal laws of Nature Forces.[1]

DEVAS.

Those great beings known to your mind as the great Devas are very mighty in isolated parts such as all mountainous places which still remain unspoiled by your ordinary human kind.

These Devas are very wonderful in their powers over the magnetic currents generated in these magnetic centres, for all Nature forces work uninterruptedly where man cannot attempt to compel or subdue their power in any act of desecration.

Your eyes have been touched by the magic of the expression of God's beauty in the colours, and the many forms of floral life in your own midst, and in such places where flower-life is loved by the inhabitants, there is a special peace, not of your own world at all, but a peace as of great understanding between man and His Maker or Father.

The Nature spirits are very prolific in their numbers, your eyes should see them, they are all about you—but perhaps it will not happen yet, we cannot yet tell, for although your vibrations are tuned-in to the great spirit of Nature on account of your intense love of all this beauty made manifest, your eyes may yet be holden, so that these sights so close to yourself may still be overlooked by yourself, even though as your hand touches these frail blossoms with loving care and admiration, there is often a small Nature spirit close at hand, who watches your expression with the greatest interest. If, one day, you sat very quiet in the midst of a bank of flowers, or in a field, perhaps your eyes would gradually see through the atmosphere and your own physical eyes would then see these engaging creatures. Be very quiet and try to remember that there

---

[1] Q. In cases of levitation do we ourselves levitate or are we taken up off our feet by unseen entities ?

A. It may be done in both ways. The highest kind is, of course, the levitation of your own physical bodies by your own powers, but there are many manifestations of levitations in which the human body is levitated by spirit entities of a not very subtle kind ; they would be those in closest contact with your own human bodies.

We could not levitate your body, but your mind could learn to levitate itself if it chose to apply itself to this very simple form of movement.

are several layers of atmosphere, and your eyes could train themselves to see these different layers, if only they were patient enough, then, when these layers have been seen or distinguished, your eyes would see that there is a position in between your atmosphere, and that this place, or dimension, is full of wonderful creatures, waiting to be seen by human eyes.

Some of them make friends with humans; they always know when they are loved and believed in; and as in all planes of existence love casts out fear, so they learn to care in their own peculiar way for their human friends, and will support them in all difficulties in ways of nature, that is to say, they will prevent mishaps amongst those who befriend them.

All fairy beings are very fond of being praised, your words vibrate on their understandings, and your admiration for their handiwork is most pleasing to them.

In the waterfalls the Nature spirits are very merry, they are full of movement, and toss the spray from one to the other, but their work is not quite so exacting as the fairies who attend to the flowers, because their work is more detailed in expression, as your brain can imagine. The water spirits are not so easy for humans to see, as they are more tenuous, and their colours very easily hidden in the colourless, or perhaps colourful, spray.

There is a very strange ritual in existence amongst these Nature spirits, and if a human ever comes into close contact with it, it may have unexpected and unexplained powers over him. This ritual is part of a worship which existed before your present human beings had entered into their human or physical bodies at all, so that your old legends about these strange doings and unseen kingdoms, these fairy rings and so forth, are all true in the world of Nature spirits, and not just idle imaginings at all. These rites are not for humans, and therefore not at all safe for them to contact in any way. It is perfectly true that it has, and does happen sometimes, that a human being has been able, quite unintentionally, to contact these secret forces and rites; the legends of country folk are full of such ideas, and they are true sometimes, but not always. There is a very thin barrier between astral entities who easily contact humans, and if the humans meddle with occult laws unwisely, or with evil intent, then strange, evil and inexplicable things may happen ; but strange things also happen when a human being, by some unexpected tuning-in to Nature spirit forces, may be admitted into unsought participation with Nature worship, not evil at all, but not understandable to the human line of evolution.

There are human beings who consciously seek and participate in such rituals ; they are very strange folk, and not to be meddled with. The ideas about witches were quite right, but of course terrible cruelty was done by those who were fearful of a witch's influence over their children, cattle, and so forth. These are quite separate in their practices from the ordinary occultists, for any human being may become an occultist at will, it is only a matter of personal endeavour and a deliberate cultivation of those psychic powers, potential in every human being, cultivated along a certain and recognized line of study, preparation, and training ; it may be perfectly pure, and in many ways will lead up to the higher degrees of spiritualism ; it may also be very evil, and degenerate into black magic ; but these ritual practices of Nature spirits and their own special Devas are quite apart in their line of evolution—magic, but not occult, as your minds understand it, and not spiritualistic at all.

These humans contact it through some very curious freak in their vibration ; probably the person would be the reincarnation of a very ancient type from the lost continents of Lemuria and Atlantis, which were full of all kinds of races not known in your present day at all.

There is no barrier between man's understanding and love of Nature in her manifestations of all kinds, whether fairies or flowers, and animals, birds, Devas, and so forth, but there are distinct acts of worship peculiar to Nature spirits, differing entirely from the homage due from man to his God. Never should man seek to participate in the ritual acts of other lines of evolution. That is where there is a danger, for an advanced occultist may indiscreetly, or wickedly, attempt to participate, and he is utterly damned if this occurs.

· You have been wondering why these fairy folk are used for work among the flowers, because your ideas have only thought of the seeds being nourished by soil and by rain and generated by the sun and the air ; but there is much more to be done than this ; each flower has an aura or etheric counterpart, and though flowers, as your eyes see them, are truly exquisite, if your eyes could see flowers as they really exist in both planes your eyes would see exquisite colours and wonderful emanations of subtle and most tenuous matter, which give the flower its share in the oversoul ; for remember, nothing can exist without that share of the oversoul, minute though that share may be ; even in your one brief vision, your eyes at once noticed the real living quality of the grass, it is quivering or vibrating with intense life, and all these meadows of flowers, which, at this moment, delight your blinded physical sight, are really quiveringly alive with a subtle life, unseen by yourself, but maintained and helped by the fairy gardeners. Each fairy has its own plant or small group of flowers to attend to, and every flower vibrates in harmony with its own special attendant.

When flowers are cultivated, then the human gardener, if he is a real gardener, supplies from his own emanation much that is good for the flowers, and the attendance of fairies is not so much given, but all flower counterparts emanated from the workshops, as it were, of the great Devas, and mankind has learnt to work in with these particular Nature forces, because there is some special note which vibrates between certain humans and their flower charges.

When flowers are cut for decoration the fairies have finished their work, and man has established a claim over their charges, so they must give them up, but there is always plenty of work for them to do, for, in addition to flowers and fruit, they have to attend to those insects who help in the propagation of the seeds for new flowers.

This unseen fairy life is truly wonderfully beautiful, and full of much labour and carefully thought-out design ; for every insect has its own work to do, and every flower is needed to carry out the vast scheme of the Great I AM.

If flowers grow in public gardens, in the quiet hours, about sunrise, there are troups of fairies visiting them. Often, in your own garden, the fairies are most busy, if your eyes could only see them, they often play round your feet, and touch your hands, as if your loving care could please them in their play.

They always work in gardens where flowers are loved and where there is much peace, and also where there are many birds, as in your own home.

Birds are most friendly with all Nature spirits, they see them, and are often used to carry these small creatures from special places to others.

Q. How are Nature spirits made and how do they increase ?

A. Through the words, or rather the vibrations of power, used by the great Devas ; a certain vibration on this particular subtle etheric matter is put into motion, and a fairy is, as it were, born ; a fairy may evaporate by the same method ; they exist accordingly as required, and as they have no individualized soul, they may be born and be disintegrated by the will of the Devas as they are required.

Q. There is a vast number of insects which destroy flowers and fruit and are a curse to mankind ; couldn't the Nature spirits keep them in better order ?

A. That, unfortunately, is part of the wrongful creation of life, brought into existence by those who tried to create without due homage to their Great God.

We have already told you that certain bad or uncontrollable forces were set free, and that at the time of this unloosing, there were certain souls who attempted to usurp powers without acknowledging their authority from God, their great Creator. They made many hideous and many destructive creatures ; and man still suffers from these faults of creative pride ; but, as time progresses, these creatures will die out or be overcome ; meanwhile man fights these enemies with pain and toil, and the spirits of Nature assist him wherever possible, for remember that there is often a wholesale slaughter of destructive insects by birds or by bigger insects, or by smaller animals, like your humble but most useful little brother mole.

Q. Do Devas create flowers ? and do they create animals ?

A. Devas act on certain lines laid down by the Great Being who is the I AM of all creation, they receive the ideas which they proceed in turn to think out, as it were, and they hand over certain details of production to their servants, the Nature spirits. But remember, the history of floral families is an ancient one and goes back many thousands of years, and Devas are always pleased to create new varieties, that is their special plan of work on etheric planes, and their servants carry out details also in subtle matter, and your physical eyes are charmed with the denser physical forms when they condense into flowers, as your minds know them. Animal life is not under Deva rule at all, but on very different lines of evolution. They have blood, and blood is the very great barrier between Deva life and physical life ; for remember, astral life is never in touch with Devas, but every animal has an astral body. Blood is a great bond between all grades of creations. Blood is very mysterious in its essence and in its power to give off mysterious fumes, which magicians used for their bestial rites and horrible lusts.

The idea of blood for sacrifice is very occult and very, very dangerous ; it arouses the worst kind of astral entities. That is why anyone turning towards a higher degree of consciousness should leave off eating meat and all really warm-blooded flesh-foods, they will keep a man back from the highest participation in the hidden wisdom.

Q. We understand there are Devas of air and water, but air and water may become storm forces of wind and rain : are these storm forces the Devas ?

A. Devas are only the spirits in charge of what is known as air and water, but not air and water in their original forces ; these become worked into storms by forces of strong magnetic current ; they are not the Devas at all ; these currents are forces, not beings at all.

Q. Are these uncontrolled forces ?

A. Yes, to a certain extent uncontrolled ; but they become so-called " uncontrolled " when still subtler forces work up strongly into magnetic currents. This is hard to explain, because magnetic currents are very far beyond human understanding ; but if you can imagine a force which is even behind these forces and in control of them, you will perhaps realize that there are forces impossible to translate into your language at all.

Q. Is man ever able to control storms, rain, wind, etc. ?

A. Yes, if sufficiently advanced in knowledge of these laws, even as your great Master Christ did, and as He also said ; but what man amongst your human kind is in possession of such advanced knowledge ? True there is a limited power among occultists, who may produce rain, and fire, and even quell wind locally, but this is a very minor operation on the scale of interference with Nature forces. These powers do not really mean control of Nature forces in the great sense, only a local affair, and this is done by persons possessing the power of touching certain Devas by vibratory contact, and not storm forces which are the great results of these magnetic storms.

CHAPTER VII

OCCULTISM

OCCULTISM, at the beginning, was the actual knowledge of natural or, as your present-day scientists would call it, very specially evolved scientific knowledge of Nature's own laws.

Occult wisdom is really knowledge which may be obtained by anyone whose mind is trained along the line of certain high vibrations, such as the way of equilibrium in space, which you would call the way of levitation. It is quite a simple law really, and makes man independent of such laws of movement as the laws which govern movement along a given straight line, the line which is sensed by dense physical bodies which have feet for this purpose.

Laws which appear contrary to laws available to the outward realization of your limited five senses are occult laws, but science is becoming aware of so-called occult laws in wireless, telepathy, television, and all laws dealing with rays, electricity, and so forth.

There is really nothing which your human bodies could not do if your knowledge were extended by knowledge which erroneously is considered occult.

When a man has trained himself to be a medium for such knowledge, he becomes superior in power to his fellow beings ; this knowledge is always awaiting those who desire it.

Occult means hidden, nothing really divine or spiritual, and the origin of occultism is really only part of man's knowledge which has been forgotten.

He had this wisdom originally, but as he became more

immersed in denser physical conditions, it was, as it were, overlaid or buried in his half-submerged mind, that which you call the subconscious mind ; it is not subconscious, but let us say submerged consciousness.

Anything which gives one man superiority over another is a source of power, and these hidden faculties became sources of power, therefore others feared those who possessed them. Knowledge is power, but the real danger is in the use of power for selfish purposes : that is the real difference between what is known as black magic and white magic.

There is nothing really evil in Nature unless used in violation of the law of Love.

There are very many co-called occult schools in your midst, schools which are not at all wise, not at all helpful, not at all useful, and many which are very evil indeed. These evil Brotherhoods as a rule exist purely for the gratification of bestiality and lust amongst certain evil human beings, whose past incarnations have possessed occult wisdom which they have profaned to their own baser uses, and of course, whenever this is done, the occultist becomes an easy prey to very undeveloped or even vile astral entities, and his pathway henceforward is one of great danger to his victims, and of most terrible penalties to his own soul in the end.

There are also very fine occult schools, which are run entirely to help mankind, and we work with many of these. Our own White Brotherhood is a very vast Brotherhood, and our members are drawn from spiritual men and women whose incarnations are, as a rule, concluded on your earth plane, and our work henceforward will always be to help all souls of all planets to progress towards their final goal of heavenly perfection on our own inner planes.

Whenever a man or woman is made a member of a true occult school, they will at once know that they are in touch with what is really spiritual and helpful, and the result will, before long, be quite tangible to their outer intelligences. On the other hand, when a man or woman becomes a member of a bad school, or of a very foolish school, they will be held by their credulity alone, and they will not make progress of a high type at all.

Occultism is a method of developing certain latent powers

within the human personality, which will render that personality able to use, what appear to be, magical means of obtaining knowledge, achieving powers, and of rendering the ordinary human body entirely subservient to this occult knowledge of hidden laws, laws quite apart from the ordinary human mind.

PSYCHISM.

Psychism is the attempt to develop certain extensions of senses, which each one possesses and could use quite legitimately for the further gathering of knowledge of that which is usually intangible to the ordinary five senses of mankind.

This is not dangerous at all if allowed to develop wisely, slowly, and always with the highest idea of ultimate spiritual growth, and so long as the person's health is not injured.

SPIRITUALISM.

Spiritualism is the knowledge through prayer, meditation and contact with beings of a much higher plane ; this never harms, but alone raises the vibrations of the individual to a complete understanding of the wondrous and beauteous future awaiting his soul in the higher planes.

Projecting the astral body is part of the training of the occultist, and has its own purpose, but do not tamper yourself with this kind of work, it may become very dangerous ; it will never help a man to become highly spiritual, though it will not hinder him either, but generally these practices are not wise.

There are certain dangers against which your minds should be guarded by knowledge which we will proceed to give you.

Know now that there are certain occult powers which exist in every human body, and which may be, and are, very much abused by the moral pervert for vile reasons, not even dimly sensed by those who are pure in bodily habits.

Whenever moral perversion takes place, certain astral entities are loosed in the midst of your own people, and those juices which are released from the body give off certain emanations which supply the matter of physical existence for these foul beings, which are evoked by these vile occultists ; they know how to use these entities, it is a vile travesty of infernal power, and rouses terrible entities, which give the most delirious sensations. This satanism is practised quite a lot by many on your earth ; it is the vilest form of pandering to the lowest astral emotions.

Now let us turn to the more pleasing aspect of occultism, for it has its great aspect also. Occultism, properly studied, has the power of linking human personalities with the personality of the universe ; this is a very curious term to use, but it really expresses what we mean as clearly as it can be expressed in your ordinary language.

Your minds have puzzled over the laws of gravitation. It is very true that gravitation is the law of the attraction of an object towards the centre point, but, from an occult point of view, gravity is not this law at all. What makes attraction ? What is there to be attracted ? That, of course, reminds you that to have sense of attraction connotes a sense of repulsion or of separation.

These are very great laws, but it is easier for a trained occultist to realize them than for those who have not studied this training. It is sufficient for each soul to realize that God, the Heavenly Father, is indeed the centre of your soul's gravity, and each soul must seek that centre by the law of love, which is the law of spiritual affinity.

This subject of occultism should not be eschewed by such as seek divine wisdom, because of its possible dangers ; for remember there is no danger to the pure in heart, for they are permitted to see God ; that is to say they are able, even in these strangely arranged laws, to understand that God is behind all laws, all wisdom, all occultism and spiritualism, for without Him nothing exists.

The real shrinking which many feel is the innate knowledge already lying in their submerged consciousness, that there may be a perversion of knowledge ; it may even be that they have already known and played with it in past lives ; but there the warning lies, and it is for all true seekers after truth to seek those things which are above, and having found the first beautiful glimmering of the light, to follow that light and never allow its radiance to be dimmed by seeking for selfish power or greedy self-emulation.

NSEEN ENTITIES.

There are disembodied entities which react on the human
mind and body, and it is really very necessary to understand
this particular form of spirit-life in connection with your
own people on earth.

Know then that there are various grades of entities
which are not human in evolution, and which often aspire
to be associated with yourselves, on account of a vicarious
enjoyment obtained in their association with the emotions
of human souls. They are not really evil beings, yet not
at all allied to anyone or anything which your minds cannot
understand. If a human being has a weakness for any
special drug, or drinks very much, or even gives way to the
effect of alcoholic fumes, then these entities, which are
purely astral, are able to attach themselves or entangle
themselves in the astral body, that is, the magnetic body
of the man or woman.

They (the human beings) enjoy certain astral vibrations
it is true, but these astral vibrations are all the while being
shared by these unpleasing entities, which often take
possession of the man or woman, and incite them to folly
or even crime, for the real soul-part of the human is swamped,
as it were, in a fog of astral emanations, and for the time
being they lose sight or knowledge of their own identity.
As the fumes wear off, these entities evaporate, as it were,
and then reunite wherever another victim is to be found.
They are nuclei of astral atoms which are not absorbed into
any special form, and as they contact the astral emanations of human beings, and only of the lower kind,
they form a definite kind of body, and possess a brief
entity of their own, but they do not evolve into definite
recognized evolving bodies ; they are like portions of
astral fog collecting and dispersing and doing harm,
because they do not belong to the higher vibrations of
astral matter.

Another kind of unseen entity is the entity that evolves
out of the mental stimulation of creatures possessing
mentality of a higher order, such as your mankind and
those which answer to mankind in other planets.

These entities can be very beautiful or very unpleasing

also, as they depend on the thoughts emanating from the minds of many varied mentalities.

Now these entities are really the progenitors of health or disease ; that is the reason why a badly trained mentality can make itself felt in illness, disease, and all kindred ills, depression, melancholia, insanity, and so forth. This mentality need not necessarily be the entire work or growth of the man's present life, it may equally well be the result of a mentality, ill-trained and unbalanced, in a previous life.

The sooner mankind begins to realize the influence of past incarnations, the sooner will mankind begin to effect sensible cures of many ills.

Now your mind can begin to understand the truth that mind controls matter, and that whatsoever a man has sown in any past that must he reap some day to the very fullest degree. No one can be too careful about his thoughts, for, whether for good or evil, a man's mental attitude towards life brings into existence certain vibratory forms which your minds call thoughts, but which have a being or existence independent of the one who thinks, the moment they are thought ; for certain vibrations are set up for weal or woe, and certain influences for health or disease are cast forth into the world to carry on an existence which will draw many within their own extending circles.

Thoughts not only vibrate in the atmosphere, they take unto themselves very definite forms, beautiful and geometrically perfect, or jagged edges and hideous, and poor in design and colour.

Q. There are surely occasions in life when anger is justifiable, in fact when it acts as a moral stimulant on those who excite it : what about these thoughts ?

A. Anger is never justifiable, though often well merited by such as are cruel, spiteful, and malicious towards their fellow beings. Justifiable anger is only justifiable from a very great Being towards an evildoer over whom that great Being may have some kind of jurisdiction.

Yet anger is not the correct word to use, for anger denotes a throwing out of a fiery emanation which destroys or injures, and no great Being really does this.

Q. Yet Christ drove out the money-changers with a whip ?

A. That is most likely true, for He is a very great Being,

and was in a position to deal out punishment to those abominable men who practised so much oppression on the weak, and profaned their religion, but who amongst you is His equal in any way ?

Leave all retribution to God and His delegates ; all will be reckoned with in the proper time. No man is sinless, therefore no man is justified in being angry with his brother.

No human can, at first perhaps, prevent hurt or injured, or even angry feelings, but he should immediately try to turn his thoughts into a very much happier channel, remembering that all men are sinful, weak, and foolish, himself no less than others.

Thus these harsh and ugly thought-forms will not be really strongly expressed enough to take shape, and the slight mental mist will disperse. It takes persistence and strongly expressed anger or hate or distrustfulness to make a real living form.

Those whose minds perpetually mistrust, or whose minds are full of malice and distrust, lies, scandalmongering, spitefulness, these are they who, being sick themselves, spread abroad their own mental sickness like a fell miasma, poisoning all who live within their auras.

Q. How should we deal with criminals ? Law and order could hardly go on tolerating such in the midst of decent people ?

A. True, but remember your courts of justice are ruled by men who maintain an attitude of indifference towards these unhappy people. They are truly impersonal, and do not punish from personal anger, but according to wisely worked ideas of government. Capital punishment is, of course, entirely wrong, and will, as years progress, cease to be practised amongst civilized races.

Learn to understand your children, they are the saints or the criminals of the future, and often a man may have been helped on his criminal path by unwisdom, or neglect, or coercion in his childhood.

Try to understand a child's tendencies ; each brings a trial from a past life to overcome, each has a debt to pay, each has certain characteristics, but do not coerce, nor crush, nor be weakly indulgent. Love and sympathy may help even the most evil reincarnated soul in the first few years of its life.

Now there are, of course, other entities whose bodies are quite apart from the human evolution, and yet which may try to contact humans at some time or other ; these are the disembodied spirits or astral bodies of the less advanced dæmons, as they were called by the Greeks ; they are of a different evolution and never seek to hurt humans, but they may seek intercourse on the astral regions when the astral or magnetic human being has laid aside the physical body, either in sleep, or in what your minds call death. They are quite beautiful, and often friendly and helpful, but have no special lasting influence on their human companions, only a passing friendliness. They never influence the physical body, they merely contact the magnetic body, much as the Nature spirits may.

Q. Are there really devils ?

A. Yes, there are very evil entities who govern the lower astral region, the terrible beings evoked by black magicians, and evoked by those who practise black occultism, the terrible black mass, or all such ghastly perversions of created beings and ceremonies.

Q. If a man who practises wrong occultism makes up his mind to injure some decent person who has opposed him and who is quite ignorant of occultism and therefore not on guard against it, can he really injure that person ?

A. Unfortunately he can, because occultism is a very deadly weapon in the hands of any unscrupulous and clever occultist.

Remember, every man has his Guide and Guardian Angel, and these can help destroy the power, but they cannot really prevent the occultist from doing a certain amount of harm. Eventually the bad man will suffer fourfold for abusing his powers, but the other man may always defend himself by prayer against enmity, only so many do not pray, and so they neglect the great shield which lies at their very feet. " Watch and pray " said your Master Christ ; truly ye know not in what hour an enemy may assail your soul.

GUARDIAN ANGELS AND GUIDES.

It is really amazing how much lies hidden from your physical senses in your ordinary life on earth ; we are full of wonder that your senses remain ignorant, and yet many of your human kind are quite sensitive to these unseen elements in your lives.

It will amaze your minds to know that, if your eyes were really opened, they would often find quite wonderful companions at your side, for each has his Guardian Angel, a being quite other than ourselves, as a Guide. Our work with yourselves much depends on the advancement of your soul's incarnations; but these Guardian Angels are always near your bodies, only their work is merely to guard rather than guide.

Guardianship means that these Beings, as far as possible, shield your entire being from as much ill as possible ; they prevent your taking undue risks very often ; but Guides are advanced spirits which have once been human also, and we make contact with your mentalities for the purpose of teaching, training, and helping on your soul's evolution.

Many Guides have links with the past lives of those they assist in their present lives, whilst Guardian Angels, as yourselves call them, have never been on the line of human evolution at all. They record a man's balance of good and evil, whereas we do nothing of that kind—we act as the elder brothers of our younger brothers, and we do all we can to make them understand how to live, so that they may more quickly pass through their earthly existences, and find work on other and higher planes.

We, ourselves, are easier to realize, because we have the power of making ourselves known in various ways, as you already know, yet these Angels may sometimes make themselves seen, especially by little children. They are spiritual entities, and work under very wonderful and very highly evolved angels—Archangels, as your Scriptures know them, the Heavenly Host.

Q. If a man is consistently evil does his Guardian Angel still remain with him ?

A. Yes, to the very end of his life, for he must have all his life recorded, and this is done by the angel alone.

Q. Has every one a definite Guide as well as an Angel ?

A. Not every one, because a Guide must always have contact with the human being, and if a man is very undeveloped from a spiritual or psychic point of view, it is naturally not much use for a Guide to attach himself or herself to this undeveloped man, unless there is, more or less, a link with the past ; but in that case the man ought to be more open to a Guide's influence.

In the case of yourself and your present circle, we are very closely in touch with yourselves, because of our link with yourself in the past, and because you have deliberately offered yourselves for work. We are definitely attached to yourselves and yourselves to us. We are one Brotherhood for the helping of humanity.

GUIDES.

Q. May we know why highly developed Guides retain their nationalities when showing themselves on this earth, not appearing just as Spiritual Beings ?

A. Let us answer your question on the subject of why we your Guides appear to preserve our own racial identities. This is a most interesting problem and we will try to render it clear to your minds.

When a human being retires from incarnation on your particular planet he is given a choice of labour in the vast scheme of the myriad universes.

As a rule we retain certain prevalent racial peculiarities and these are peculiar to the Archetypal form of our individualization as man.

Each race has its own peculiar part to play in the scheme of human life ; just as every great religion has its own special message to the world in general, so has each race a special duty to the race of man in general.

There is no real distinction of colour, caste, or creed, as your more advanced souls know well, and your Guides are attracted to your present incarnate selves because of your own links with the remote past, or because our vibrations tune-in with certain psychic qualities in your own make-up. The higher in vibration the human mind is as a receiving-station, the more advanced the vibration of the Guide, and the more spiritually or higher-mentally developed the degree of consciousness which is established between ourselves and yourselves.

Your white races are much younger in history and information than the real Indian, the ancient Chinese or Egyptian. That is why the more advanced Guides usually appear in these outward bodies.

There are as yet not very many white Guides whose work is of very outstanding importance, although there are very many most spiritually-minded spirits of the white races who help us in our contact with modern life. They act as intermediaries as a rule, and in time will become just as wise and highly evolved as the older races in wisdom and knowledge, but not yet.

CHAPTER VIII

ASTROLOGY

Planetary Influences. Law of Periodicity. Free Will. The Horoscope.

It is very customary to regard astrology purely from the aspect of the telling of general characteristics, and the prophesying of certain events in the life of the person whose horoscope is being cast ; yet there is a far higher aspect of astrology, for as there are certain evolutions of planets in your solar system, so there are certain affinities between your individual aspect of planetary influence, and the planetary influences playing upon your earth, your country, your race, your family, and your own self.

The laws which govern the science of astrology are the laws of periodicity, and just as certain aspects of planets bring certain aspects of vibrations to bear at certain recurring periods of what your minds call time, so is the whole of your mankind influenced to a certain extent by certain recurring aspects of these influences in a smaller or greater degree.

It is, of course, very difficult to understand how these influences work, for they are governed by cosmic laws and there is no recovery from these cosmic laws if your own soul has elected to be reincarnated in certain aspects, in which there will be certain malefic influences.

If a machine is set in motion, a machine which tears or grinds, and at a certain point a fly deliberately sets itself in the way of that machine, that machine will crush it without doubt ; so that if your soul has chosen a certain aspect of planetary influences, which will work out relentlessly and without hesitation—for cosmic laws are relentless—then your physical body will certainly be caught in those influences.

It is the soul which has free choice, free will—not the

body. The body is the servant of the soul. You think this a fatalistic idea ; it is not fatalistic really, for the soul has only chosen influences which will prove the best training for itself, and in that training it may be successful or not, just as the type of human character allows ; but the soul, sometime or other, will have to face those planetary influences, and be raised triumphant or enter again into incarnation.

Man may always rise superior to any unhappy or unfortunate circumstances, but he may not evade them ; he may overcome unfortunate tendencies in his own character brought over from past lives ; he may forge new chains, or cast off old fetters ; his fate is in his own hands, but the method of his trial is clearly indicated by the hour which the soul chooses for its descent into your physical world again.

Now the law of periodicity is a very strange law and a very far-reaching law ; for every kind of manifestation is caught regularly and at set times into certain cycles of manifestation, and as souls are bound to meet each other during certain incarnations, these cycles are wide in extent, but always mathematically precise in their working out in all grades of material.

Your mind is familiar with the twelve signs of the Zodiac, and if correctly understood from the inner aspect, much wisdom may be given the soul (or rather the physical brain) with regard to events and characteristics belonging to every sign. The actual pictures of your present Zodiac are not the original symbols at all, for these existed on the old Atlantean continent, and much more was understood in those times about this great cosmic law than your present civilization has ever understood.

The horoscope is a chart for your journey through each incarnation, but there are remarkably few astrologers of your own age whose knowledge is more than extremely superficial. The real horoscope could and should tell all past incarnations, and indicate with accuracy the future pathway which should be followed by the soul in its present incarnation ; that is divine wisdom, and that is the highest kind of astrology.

Your minds ask how it could be possible, because the stars or planets, which the astrologers tell you influence your lives, are only stars or heavenly bodies a very long way off ; but these planets are not these heavenly bodies at all, they are great luminous cosmic entities by which certain manifestations were brought into being, under the will of your heavenly Father. They rule certain cycles of time, and send forth certain rays at certain rates of vibration, and their combination of rays and of vibrations sets up forms which are inhabited by certain portions of soul-essence sent out from the great oversoul. So that perhaps your minds can catch a glimmer of the truth of forms inhabited by soul-essence, emanating from certain rays or junction of rays, vibrating to certain vibrations, tuning-in with certain aspects of creation, and finding affinities in all grades of material representation in all kingdoms of Nature.

Now can you understand even yet another vista of the manner in which all creation travails together in the bondage of cosmic birth, under the law of periodicity. This will be sufficient for our book. We merely wish to indicate the truth of this despised science : it is a wonderful science, and should be much more carefully studied.

CHAPTER IX

SYMBOLISM

The Secret Language. The Point within the Circle. Attraction and Repulsion. Four Elemental Kingdoms. The Solid Angle. The Cross. The Cross of Christ. The Ankh. The Swastika. The Spiral.

SYMBOLISM is the universal, hidden, and secret language, for all symbols are equal in expression in all races, in all ages, in all languages ; they stand for certain fundamental ideas in the mental oversoul or mind of the Great Creative Forces, which in their turn have emanated from the Mind of God, the Great Being, the I AM, the root of all expression and of all beings in all planes of existence.

It is very necessary to start, as in your simple geometry, with the point within the circle, but this is already explained in your chapter on numbers.[1] Nevertheless the point within the circle is the symbol of all symbols, for none can exist, or be expressed in any way without this point, which, besides being the symbol of GOD HIMSELF, expresses a point of place or position in the Cosmos, which is necessary before any construction of further ideas may be conceived at all.

Now this point or centre stands for beginning, source, being, existence, and all these immense and unexplainable ideas. It is very remarkable that the smallest possible symbol is the real and only symbol of all that is too immense even for contemplation to the ordinary mind, even to our slightly more advanced minds also.

Having established our beginning, we proceed to think what is the force contained within this point or centre, for remember, it must be the source of all forces whatsoever they may be. The point expresses that which IS, and what IS must be further extended, or the point would remain static and no development would be possible ; so that within this point there is a further power—a power of

[1] See p. 20.

movement—that which IS extends into that which expresses movement, and hence your minds see at once the establishment of two forces, a force which leaves the centre, and because all existence must always remember its progenitor or projector (existence presupposes a memory of expulsion from a parent or a beginning), then the other force begins to dawn upon our mental faculty, and we recognise the force of attraction.

So then, from the centre, which is the beginning and the end, the ALPHA and OMEGA (as it is expressed in your scriptures), your minds can visualise these two forces springing out, one of repulsion—that is centrifugal—and one of attraction, or drawing in again—the centripetal.

Now we are not going to say these two forces form a right angle, because they do not, but they do form a line, and that line may go in any direction. So long as it issues from the centre it is the law of attraction that helps to form this straight line, in fact draw a point, and then send a line expressing expulsion or repulsion.

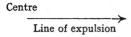

Centre

Line of expulsion

Now draw a centre and a line to express attraction.

Centre

Line of attraction

Your eyes can now understand that the line is only one line after all, there is no question of a right angle so far, is there ?

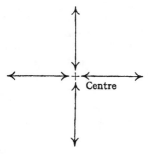

Centre

Now if your mind draws a centre with lines of attraction and repulsion in four directions, another idea will dawn.

F

Now your mind sees that right angles can only be imagined by sending lines of attraction and repulsion in all directions on a plane surface, so that in your last figure your mind gives the picture of a cross, and the four lines give the four directions and they are typical of the four elemental kingdoms, for these forces exist in each elemental kingdom naturally, for they are the forces at the foundation of all expression or materialization.

Now let us proceed with this question of a right angle, which can only be formed by the union of two of these four lines.

Again draw this plane surface figure of the cross, and name each with one of the four names—air, fire, water, earth. Place fire in the North, air in the South, water in the West, and earth in the East.

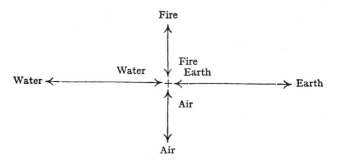

Now if your eyes rest on the parts where each line meets at the centre, you will see that there is a very interesting place of meeting.

They all meet on the centre, and as each kingdom is of a different density, then you can surely see that the centre already begins to differentiate its own material essence, and gives off matter in these various degrees of density ; so that the plane surface is no longer flat, but has thickness, throughness, solidity, call it what your mind cares to call it, but existence is no longer shown as a symbol of one or even two dimensions, for the centre has become a whorl of everincreasing density.

Now draw it in this way—take the centre and confine it with a circle make the four dimensions.

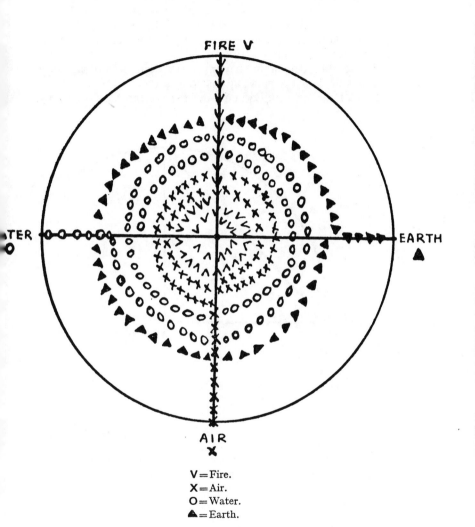

V = Fire.
X = Air.
O = Water.
▲ = Earth.

Now your mind has begun to understand throughness from the centre with its four dimensions or directions; always remembering that there is nothing flat, although for the sake of rendering ideas intelligible to the human intelligence they have to be drawn flat.

Remember, the four elemental kingdoms are really only degrees of density, varying considerably of course in vibration and in their individual powers of expression—and by

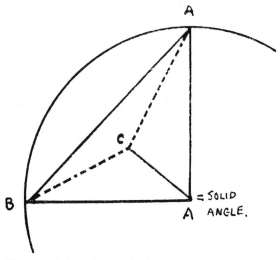

Diagram of the Solid Angle shown in the flat containing all degrees of density.

expression we mean typical creations on each of these kingdoms.

The right angle is made by the point in drawing where these forces of the varying kingdoms meet. Do not think of flat angles, but of solid angles.

Now try to think of this angle as having all parts of the fourfold kingdom contained in itself, that is to say—the right angle really gives that point where all four kingdoms meet, so that at the centre there is no real distinction on the flat surface portrayed by your flat angle, but a living throughness in all degrees of density emanating from the centre which is all things.

The meeting place in the centre is the right angle actually. Now if you can remember that all right angles are typical of expression of the Absolute on all kingdoms of material expression, you can quite easily see that the right angle in its solid aspect is typical of the great force of creation on all planes of matter, and that the cross in the circle is the vast emblem of creation in every aspect of expression.

The Cross is a cosmic symbol, and is a very ancient symbol even among your own mankind ; much of the mystery teaching is contained within its four arms.

We have shown how the Cross began to be enclosed in the circle, but so that there be no error, let us recapitulate. The Centre is God the Absolute, the very beginning of all things ; then the extension brings about a state of duality, or divine marriage with the existing illimitable space or chaos ; and hence through the union of what is positive, or projective, or dynamic, into what is negative, or receptive, or static, a state of form-manifestation becomes possible ; but because manifestation exists on all four planes of manifested kingdoms or existences, this is symbolised by the projection of lines from the centre in four different directions, equidistant and mathematically precise—hence the Cross with arms or straight lines extending North, South, East, and West.

However, it becomes necessary for the human mind to make some limit to the limitless, and because that also must be mathematically precise, a circle taken from the centre, or absolute, is described, cutting these extended arms at exactly the same point in each extension into space.

Now let us proceed with this same symbol, for the Cross is given in a variety of methods of drawing, and each has its own particular meaning, for just as the Cross of equal arms denotes the Great All, the Limitless Limited, so this great mystery cannot be expressed in language of words, it is only possible in a symbol, for then all minds will grasp the great Truth.

The Cross of Crucifixion is not the same in manifestation, but it is typical of man, in this way, that a man standing erect with arms extended represents the man archetypal standing on the earth (or densest matter), with head erect and arms expanded to denote freedom, also a giving up of all limitations, whether of the self, or of the limits of physical joys and sorrows ; he is detached from all that would hold him, he gazes upwards towards his own heavenly home, and is in a position neither abased nor suffering, but strong, upright, and joyous in his knowledge of his own inherent divinity ; his body is a symbol in all its parts of the universe ; he is composed of all the various constituents of the cosmos ; he is indeed the microcosm, a miniature of the macrocosm.

So now we have the cosmic cross and the microcosmic cross, which is also the cross of Initiation ;[1] for just as man is the type of the universe in miniature, so is his journey through his innumerable lives (until he obtains this mystical knowledge) portrayed in this crucifixion, a spiritual being, placed symbolically on the cross of matter, in recognition of his own particular evolution in the denser world of experiences.

At this moment in his initiation he has attained the knowledge of spiritual union with the densest matter, and such knowledge is only possible to him who will " go out no more," as it is written in your own scriptures.

Never forget, the cross of freedom, not the cross of dreadful suffering, is the cross of the Christ Consciousness ; for the Cross of Christ—that is the Cross as a symbol of Christ Consciousness—is indeed the cross of At-One-Ment, not of atonement, as your priests tell your people. It denotes a tremendous advance in spiritual knowledge when a man shall truly say : " This, my soul, has lain on the cross of at-one-ment, and I, the human entity, have seen my own salvation in the tomb of renunciation ; I am ascended into the highest heaven of spiritual knowledge, and perfectly realize that I am one with my Heavenly Father."

This mystery teaching is not yet fully understood in your own Christian Churches, and it is our special wish that this teaching shall be sent out into your world in this our new mystical book written in your hand.

Give these words as your mind receives them, and be not afraid of angry protests, for this is the truth of the Cross and it must be taught now.

[1] See p. 32.

THE ANKH.

There are other cross symbols, the ANKH, as given in our
own Egyptian writings, and this is not quite the same in
its teaching as these other crosses.

The Ankh is the sign of union between that which is male
and that which is female, and therefore it is a sign of pro-
creation, preservation, manifestation, and of generation
and regeneration ; that it became a sign of bestiality later
in its history is of course only a sad example of man's
depravity through misuse of these powers of generation ;
but in the beginning the Ankh was a symbol of the highest
idealism of the mystery of cosmic sex functions, which were
later misapplied by man at his worst.

THE SWASTIKA.

The Swastika is the next Cross to be considered. It is
not entirely understood, because it is more than a symbol
of periodicity or recurrence, it is a symbol of divine energising
power, and as it is drawn in connection with the cosmic
cross, that is, it has equal arms though no circle, it is the
symbol of cosmic existence in divine energy ; it is the
symbol of universal manifestation in perpetual movement
or vibration ; it is the symbol of divine breathing-out, and
therefore, whereas the Ankh is the sign of generation, so the
Swastika is a symbol of the divine spirit, the all-pervading
breath of GOD THE ONE, THE BEGINNING AND THE END.

THE SPIRAL.

Now let us go on a step further, and discuss the symbol
of the Spiral.

This symbol is found in every kind of place, in every
type of manifestation, in fact, all progress is a spiral, and
hence the spiral is the symbol of evolution in all planes of
existence. The true spiral begins from a small whorl and
gradually increases in circumference or girth, or the better
word is extent.

Imagine the Centre (and remember no symbol can start
without this centre), and from this Centre, which is Life,
issues life Essence. Now that which is essence cannot be
expressed to the human mind as a mathematically precise

figure like an angle or a square. Essence suggests a loosely woven or cloudy emanation, fluid or gaseous ; this essence is projected, whether in a dense cloud or tenuous one, it takes on a shape of rings of ever widening extent, just as a pebble thrown in a pond causes ever widening rings of movement on the surface, so these sparks of Divine Life or Energy, sent off from the Great Centre, depart into what we must call space, and as they go they cause rippling or vibratory clouds ; as they pursue their course there is apparently no mathematical precision in their work, yet every turn of the spiral, every ripple of vibration bears a perfect proportion to the preceding ripple or vibration.

Yet even in this spiral there is an angular mathematical precision as in every design in all manifested nature, in all true art, and in man himself.

We were considering the spiral as a symbol of evolution, and that is perfectly correct, for the spiral suggests a gradual evolving in space in rhythm and convolutions ; no strictly lineal ascent or descent, but a gentle and flowing movement, gradual and in due proportion through all densities of matter up to the very centre pivot, or outward and downwards into untold diversity, and at every turn and twist of the upward or downward gradation the triangle, with its two right angles, is implied.

CHAPTER X

SYMBOLISM (*contd.*)

Platonic Solids. The Tetrahedron. The Pyramid. The Octahedron. The Icosahedron. The Cube. The Dodecahedron. First Causes. Fire. Air. Water. Earth.

PLATONIC SOLIDS.

Now all symbols of a Cosmic nature are to be found within the five platonic solids ; all designs are founded on them, also all schools of thought may be traced back to this very wonderful system, which was systematised by the Master Pythagoras, but it was already common knowledge amongst all Initiates.

It is very necessary to understand, first of all, that these figures are not symbols of concrete matters appertaining to your earth planet at all, but symbols expressing abstract ideas in your own gross material world. Symbolism is the only possible language, for when the soul endeavours to express all that is known to it in the higher realms, it is immediately stopped for lack of a language in terms of actual speech, so that it is forced to draw certain symbols or designs, which shall convey as far as possible that which appertains to the Cosmos or world of abstract ideation.

These five figures represented to the earlier schools of the time of the great Master Pythagoras, the most simple and yet the most perfect ideas of what was fundamental to all manifested creation on the dense planes of your own material earth.

He conceived that all manifestation issued from five graduations of material, one denser than the other, if they were regarded from the beginning, or each one finer—that is to say, more attenuated—than the last, if counted from the densest to the finest.

Fire was not fire, as your minds understand it : that which warms, burns, destroys. Fire was the Cosmic or ultra-divine energy which caused manifestation to ignite. Fire, in other words, was celestial or divine ignition.

Now when this idea was put into a term of speech, it was quite impossible to make man understand fire apart from its destructive faculty, even though man was fully aware of its warming, invigorating faculty as well. Therefore it was reserved apart from earthly symbolism by using a geometrical one, the symbol known as the Tetrahedron, the four triangles all joining together, forming, what your minds call, a solid ; that is, something which conveys an impression of what we must call *throughness*.

These four triangles were meant to express to the human mind that celestial ignition is a quality which permeates all four types of bodily formation, not only in the universe, but in man's own body—for there is divine ignition or energy in the etheric, in the magnetic, in the mental and in the physical body.

This will be explained in our chapter on the human constitution.[1] Remember also that every triangle has two right angles, and every right angle gives the two forces in Nature—attraction and repulsion, positive and negative, and so forth ; it is necessary to have two points of ignition, one is to lead the mind into abstract idea, the other into concrete form. This figure expresses most simply and eloquently the presence of the Divine Fire on all planes of matter, even in the four bodies of man himself.

Spiritually, this idea was adopted as the great symbol of religious thought, for spiritual life exists only so far as the man's soul is aware of the divine ignition, inspiration, or light, within its own centre of being, hence the great religions have always chosen LIGHT as a special symbol of the Divine Presence.

Now with regard to the next figure, the Octahedron, this again is of triangular form, for all these manifestations of abstract idea were conveyed through a triangle, which again always possesses two right angles, which in their turn give the primary idea of ignition, concrete and abstract.

Now the air is a very subtle element ; it permeates all the heavier planes of existence, and is of very highest

[1] Page 108.

importance, for it is as much part of the life of the heavier
planes as of the more subtle, hence the symbol expresses
divine permeation above, below, and throughout—four
triangles on an imaginary four-sided base, set in opposition
to a corresponding four triangles suspended from the above
figure. That, again, is not air as the human mind understands it, but air the force or law of penetration.

The Pyramid, as your minds see it now, is a four-triangled
figure on a four-sided base. Half the Octahedron, yet not
the Tetrahedron ; why is this ? That is a very subtle
question. The Tetrahedron was the figure used in the
remoter period of Temple building, but is not known to your
present mind at all. The Pyramid was built on a later idea,
and is meant to represent the four elemental kingdoms on
a base of four equal sides. The symbolism is quite correct,
but not so perfectly carried out as in the figure of the
Octahedron ; the Pyramid leaves the abstract half of the
figure to the imagination, the Platonic solid expresses its
completion.

All triangular forms give expression of abstract ignition.
The introduction of a square gives the idea of permeation
or abstract breath.

Then we come to the third, which is water, the Icosahedron.

We have considered ignition, permeation, and now we
consider the principle of division, or coming away from.

We have already told you that water is a symbol of the
great divider in Nature's kingdom, but water is not quite
what your minds have thought it ; it is the heavy portion
of elemental essence ; it is air condensed, remember, and
condensed through heat, so that even in your ordinary
process your own watery kingdom depends on fire and air.
It is therefore the third of the triangular series of figures.

Now try to imagine what the shape of an Icosahedron
suggests to your mind. It is beginning to suggest a ball as
your eyes look at it, that is, a spherical figure, a circle,
so that very soon your mind will have reached that
which formed only on a centre is the symbol of the
universe.[1]

But we hasten too fast. Water is the third position in the
Cosmic symbols, the natural sequence, and though it

[1] i.e. the Dodecahedron.

irrigates, purifies, satisfies in its physical embodiment, it also divides.

Can you not see by degrees how true is the axiom " God Geometrises ? " First on Cosmic lines, then on the lines of separate development (as in the case of man's own self)—always form built on number or geometrical forms.

Water, then, is the divine irrigator, the universal fluid, and its form in the Icosahedron begins to suggest the circle.

We will next consider the square or cube, the plane surface figure and the solid, for both mean much the same idea.

As a symbol of earth, it is not, of course, what your mind terms the earth, that is your own planet, nor the soil ; nor the heavier cohesive mass of atoms which form the denser bodies of manifestation, that is flesh, as in the case of animal life, the accumulation of cells forming bodies whether of your animal, vegetable, or mineral kingdom. But earth, as understood by the higher consciousness, is that animated mass of individualities forming a complete body or whole, and therefore something which is a solid or crystallized mass, with very distinct appendages on all other planes, each body composed of fire, air, water, and crystallization—a fourfold being which has to be denoted by a cube.

The cube is a symbol of forms in material sheaths, not necessarily man or any special form, but form in a body of some kind of dense matter, form possessing material life.

The symbol of man is not in these solids, for the Dodecahedron, which is the highest and most complete, gives the symbol of perfected form, in which the divine breath or ether is the all-pervading part. The Dodecahedron is a symbol of the completed universe, formed of divine fire, air, water, earth, and held together by some very subtle body, called by your own people by the name of ether, which is not quite the ether which we know, which was in the beginning the breath of God, by which man and all creation became living soul.

So now in brief your minds have achieved a slight knowledge of these platonic solids, for they are the symbols which are at the base of all true symbolism.

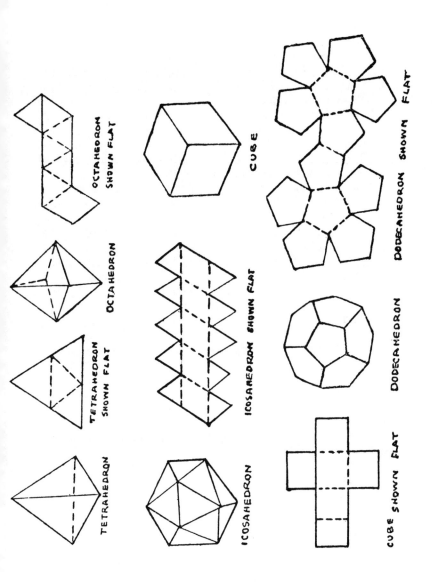

OCTAHEDRON SHOWN FLAT

OCTAHEDRON

TETRAHEDRON SHOWN FLAT

TETRAHEDRON

CUBE

ICOSAHEDRON SHOWN FLAT

ICOSAHEDRON

DODECAHEDRON SHOWN FLAT

DODECAHEDRON

CUBE SHOWN FLAT

Q. You said vibration made certain forms ?

A. Truly vibration is a most difficult subject to impart to your physical brains, because one question after another will arise in your minds, and we cannot always convey the truth however much we may wish to do so.

Vibration implies energy, and that is correct, because all things emanate through energy, Cosmic or Divine, whichever your minds may choose to call it. Now when this energy is set into extra quick motion, certain forms are struck out into space. What is struck out into space continues vibrating at a certain rate, gathering momentum until it is caught into a form, and often split up into myriads of forms. This is how worlds are made.

Now vibrations may be controlled by certain instruments, either natural instruments or mediums, or by mechanical ones also.

The vibration which caused the moulding of a man was exactly the same to start with as that which caused a mountain to become a mass of vegetation or a volcano. Cosmic energy is not discriminating, but the decisive factors as to form and so forth lie in the care of the gods appointed to rule over these many series of creations.

The Cosmic dynamo may cause an earthquake, or the ripple on a pond ; it depends on the instrument tuned-in to receive its energy. Colour, light, sound, all these parts of this Cosmic energy depend, for their particular divisions into varieties of colour, light, and sound, on the instruments prepared to receive them. The receivers are prepared by the agents ruling their particular form of evolution, and a kind of reaction is set up in the recipient and the form is decided.

FURTHER TEACHING ON PLATONIC SOLIDS.

The basis of all universal religion is symbolism, and the basis of all symbolism is hidden in the Platonic Solids. Such was the language of the most ancient teachers of the finest religions your world has known, and, of course, these figures become familiar to all who study Greek thought, the basis of all the highest modern ideas of existence, pure and undefiled. In your own times also they appear in your

most modern representation of mystery teaching—in
Freemasonry.

Now these ideas of these Five bodies embodied truths
of the most far-reaching order, no less, in fact, than the basis
of first causes of creation, emanation and evolution, for
your minds must be fully aware that the merely superficial
teaching of ordinary one-lifed growth and final one-bodied
salvation, as taught to-day in your Christian churches,
does not really satisfy the intelligences of your more advanced
seekers after God.

Let us therefore attempt to give your minds some further
light on a subject which so aptly expresses these colossal
and far-reaching universal and cosmic truths.

Your diagrams can furnish your eyes with certain aspects
on a flat surface, and it is, of course, not easy to understand
or imagine these flat surfaces from a solid or through
aspect.

Let us remember that a solid angle denotes the combined action of two fundamental forces focussed on a
centre—the centre which is the Absolute, the Essence of
All.

Now these forces are alone responsible for manifested
life, as your physical brains understand it, forces which
denote perpetual energy, and perpetual desire, that is the
whole history of creation in all cases of existence. Perpetual
Energy is the Positive Force, and Perpetual Desire the
Negative Force, the Absolute possesses *both* in HIMSELF ;
He moves forever in a wave or spiral of energy, ever increas-
ing as it describes the outer whorls of movement, and He
desires to be multiplied in variety of form, so that in His
Own Divine Ideation, Energy and Desire already exist ; but
in a measure, He depended on the sending forth of those
two forces from His own undivided Self—the Centre as it is
symbolised—and Himself generated two emanations—the
Energy, or Divine Male Force, and the desire of reception
or conception, which is the Divine Female Force ; so that
from that centre the two forces, emanating from the Absolute,
became the types of Eternal Male and Eternal Female—
types which are to be found in every class of created form.

Now reduce this to a diagram. Take your centre
A————B. Here we have the point and the line—
the one has become two ; but this straight line would go

on indefinitely were it not bounded or limited, so draw a line from B downwards.

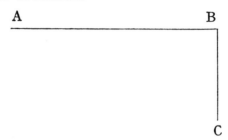

Now, having set this limit, we know that the Absolute has expressed (1) Energy, and (2) Limitation. Now let us consider this point ; this limitation gives your mind the first indication of form, for form is the receptacle of Divine Idea in the limitation of a form. Do you not see that at the end of line B, your other line of limitation has given your brain the drawing of a right angle, so that the right angle exists not on the original centre, which is of course untouchable, but it exists in another centre depending on the first, but a centre which quite clearly expresses the union of Energy and Form, that is, as your brains call it, Spirit and Matter.

Now let us continue this diagram : call your other end of line B, C ; so now we have a right angle A, B, C, with an *original* centre A, but with a *visible* centre B. Now this is only a flat surface right angle, and there can be nothing so foolish as a flat surface in reality, for the whole of existence is solid or throughness, therefore your right angle should have lines in all directions and everywhere in your diagram your mind can see that there are right angles, and, because of this throughness, your minds must imagine a solid angle, that is, something which extends in all directions, and which is bounded on all sides by regular mathematical precision.

So far we have established our right angles in all directions, and as on another occasion we spoke of the Cosmic Cross,[1] your minds need not at this juncture consider these four divisions in that form.

Let us rather consider Fire, Air, Water, Earth, and, of course, Ether, from the Inner or celestial point of view.

[1] See p. 86.

FIRE.

Fire expresses, and is, Divine Energy, life-giving and energizing all form into expression of Divine Ideation. Fire energizes all the three elemental kingdoms, and as it is necessary to enclose your flat right-angle with a line which gives a triangle, in order to make that form solid or through, a Tetrahedron is the form necessary to express fire in its all-pervading activity.

So fire equals Divine Ignition (that is energy) on all grades of fundamental matter, and is rightly described by this symbol of the Tetrahedron.

Having established His Divine Energy the GREAT ABSOLUTE proceeds to let this celestial energy reproduce itself in varying forms, and of course in varying degrees of matter, but remember, not matter as your human understandings think of it.

AIR.

Next this celestial fire has reproduced itself in Air, for Divine Energy is not Breath, but becomes or generates Breath, and this Divine Breath is what is called Air, again celestial Air, remember.

At this point let us remember that Air is very necessary to the whole of sentient life on all planets, and if Divine Fire energizes, forms, and gives them living power, then Air is the denser power which it generates ; for remember also that generation always denotes the expression in a denser form of that which exists in the mind of the generator, so that celestial fire generates that which is denser, that is —Air.

Thus we have Fire, which generates the Air, which generates Water, and Earth or crystallization, the whole summed up into a body which is called the Dodecahedron— the sum of all those angles which originally started from the ABSOLUTE POINT or CENTRE.

G

CHAPTER XI

SYMBOLISM (*contd.*)

Platonic Solids, their relation to Universal or Nature Forces. Attunement. Human Evolution follows a distinct and separate line. The Law of Focus. Water Symbol of division.

NATURE Forces are very strong forces, and very strangely attached to certain temperamental changes in the human aura.

Your mind reacts very strongly to Nature Forces under favourable conditions. There is a certain sympathy between the human magnetic body and the magnetism of Nature. Those who seek the quiet places of your earth, and those whose whole being revolts against noise and turmoil and too much human companionship, are those whose attunement is most nearly akin to the great natural forces of wind, water, storm, sunshine, and all the manifold manifestations of the sub-human kingdoms.

It is, perhaps, very hard to realise that all these creatures and all these conditions are quite apart from the evolutionary laws which govern yourselves.

Scientists have linked all classes together, and in effect, from a certain aspect, thay have a certain amount of methodical information which is applicable to the cell bodies but not to the intelligent bodies of all physical structures.

The cells of the amœbae are constructed as human cells may be, yet there is no kinship spiritually between these lower forms of physical cell life and human cell life. Side by side, your bodies, and the bodies of your animals and birds, and the bodies of your trees and plants display themselves, yet there is a very wide gulf between all of these lives, and your trees never become your dogs, and your dogs never become yourselves, and certainly your monkeys have never been yourselves.

This idea came into being when the souls, which were never originally intended for dense physical bodies, were suddenly cast into them, and all true knowledge of soul evolution from the great OVERSOUL became involved in this present idea—that soul was something which arose from the dead or inorganic matter, rather than that of the descent of the soul material into the hell of denser material.

You can very easily see that it would be difficult to separate all these various kingdoms into their rightful divisions, unless man's mind understood that all life is run on lines peculiar to its own special development.

Here are the four recognized divisions or elemental kingdoms which man's mind has always recognized, and for which there have always existed special symbols.[1] They are the kingdoms of Earth or Solid matter (so-called), Air or Gaseous matter, Fire or Heat matter, and Water or Fluid matter, and in each of these elemental kingdoms there exist laws, ministers, and special inhabitants visible to your eye, and invisible to your eye also.

AIR.

Let us first write about the Air, for here we deal with perhaps the most difficult of all, the last to become conquered, as your scientists say, though, as a matter of fact, your human minds, brains and bodies have conquered none of these kingdoms.

At best your bodies and minds or brains are only able to learn the simplest rules appertaining to the being able to contact certain visible aspects of them, so that your bodies learn how to move in them, instead of remaining in a state of inertia. With regard to their so-called physical aspect, air, in the ordinary acceptance of the term, has no physical aspect, for though your bodies are conscious of air, and though your scientists have been able to measure, separate, and engage the properties peculiar to several gaseous substances, your minds are not properly in touch with air, any more than with ether, or any of the finer vibrations which interpenetrate yourselves, your earth plane and the universe in general.

[1] See Platonic Solids, p. 89.

Now there are laws which, of course, govern all these subtle vapours, gases, and so forth ; laws, some of which are recognized, but many of which are not yet. Your law of gravitation is a law of the air elemental kingdom, but so little do your minds know about it that your bodies are still unable to levitate, and all that is known of this power has either been left as an impracticable legend, or, as in the case of recent scientific discoveries, left severely out of common practical usage.

With vast machines your mankind clumsily imitates the birds, yet it would be quite possible for anyone who understood this law properly to move his own body at will in any direction without mechanical aid. It is a law of focussing. The mind focusses itself on any given point, and the body obeys the propelling action of that focussing.

It is simple to project the astral body ; but the physical one could also be projected. Your minds have been puzzled often by the finding of great stone monuments on positions beyond the lifting power of modern mechanical appliance, such as the pyramids and those very ancient menhirs and so forth. These were focussed into position by those who possessed this knowledge ; this was an ancient Masonic secret, for these monuments and temples were built in the ancient days of real craft wisdom and all craft wisdom was originally learnt from those Initiates who were in charge of those buildings for their own ceremonial uses.

When uses became abuses, then this knowledge (which had only been given in symbols or by words) suddenly ceased ; there was a confusion of tongues ; words of power became jumbled words of little meaning, and creative Masonry or Architecture on divine designs became an art and craft of the forgotten civilizations. These words will strike a familiar chord in the minds of certain of your readers.

From considering the air, we have quite unconsciously dropped into the consideration of solid or earth forms, but we must return to those who inhabit the air.

Your eye follows the birds in their flight, the butterflies, the bees, and all the thousands of inhabitants or users of the elemental air kingdom. We have already written about the fairies, and we have also told your mind that Devas or ruling spirits or guides exist who control all these visible and invisible creations and who have no connection with humanity in any way whatever.

Yet just as the souls of mankind were focussed or propelled into earthy forms or moulds, so is the human being a part-inhabitant of the elemental air kingdom, by reason of the subtler body of the soul being caught into manifestation by this law of gravitation and also by the laws of repulsion and attraction.

.   .   .   .   .   .

When we wrote of the elemental kingdom of air, we were aware that a certain reserve of material information would be entailed, as we cannot put into words these facts which relate to such a subtle matter ; that is the reason the Greeks worked these elemental kingdoms out as symbols, in the platonic solids. The air symbol was the eight-sided figure, because the air is tangible in all these dimensions, and the figure suggests a solid or substance which is tangible and yet sensible or visible in all these further extensions of space. " The wind bloweth where it listeth, and thou canst not tell whence it cometh, nor whither it goeth," yet it is something, some being, some essence, some material, which permeates many dimensions. Strange that your brains can only imagine three, though there are four so clearly connected with your own physical selves, that your brains might very easily sense this fourth, yet in the kingdom of the air there are very much greater extensions of dimensions, and it is impossible to touch this kingdom at all in your present consciousness.

It is, of course, very hard for the ordinary mind to realize the purpose of the Greeks in choosing these symbols to express these kingdoms of elementary forces. It is all a question of numbers, and the understanding that actually life in its entirety presents many sides to those that understand, and can see beyond the narrow limits of three-dimensional space.

EARTH.

Earth is represented by the square, that is the four-dimensional figure, and of course this does not refer to your earth planet, which is usually depicted as a globular shape, not entirely round, of course. It refers more particularly to that part of manifestation which deals with denser life forms or physical bodies ; so that here to begin with, your brains instinctively recognize a fourth dimension, which is not actually sensible to the cruder outer senses, but this fourth dimension is the link of the physical manifestation to the invisible worlds or planes—the soul plane as it were.

FIRE.

Now, of course, the fire symbol is the tetrahedron—the pyramid—the three-sided figure on the four-sided base, and just as the fire symbol teaches that all inspiration issues from the apex of a trinity it is easy to see that in this symbol of the tetrahedron or pyramid, there is a true symbol of divine essence descending into matter, and fire is the moving, warming, invigorating elemental kingdom, without which all manifestation would lose its energy and vitality, and be non-existent except as matter devoid of energy.

WATER.

Now with the symbol of water, that is the icosehedron, your mind was much troubled, because your brain was considering water in your ordinary physical sense, but water in connection with the platonic theory, that is, water considered as an elemental kingdom, is not water as your minds make it understood to your brains in the water of oceans, rivers, and so forth, but water as the fluid of universal extent, something held together by forces unknown in your own world. Water in its occult sense is not water as your bodies know it, but as it is understood in the higher spheres, where it is alluded to as the great divider of life conditions.

The four rivers of Eden are the four main divisions of Cosmic life-force, not liquid rivers at all.

Water is used in baptism for a dividing symbol, as well as a purifying one, for water divides or separates that which is pure from that which is not pure, and in baptism the new influences which divide the new life from the old life are actually the elemental substance known as water. The washing away of sins is a symbolical reference to the separation of the new soul life from the old soul life—a removal or divider.

PART II

MAN

" God created man in His own image."
" What is man that Thou art mindful of him ? "

CHAPTER XII

THE CONSTITUTION OF MAN

(a) *The Infant. Sex. The Aura.*

THE HUMAN BODY.

We are going to tell your mind some things about the human body and how it is made with its various unseen portions.

As your brain knows, you have the physical envelope with its framework of bone, muscle, and its wonderful nervous organization, which is the real part of contact with the psychic body.

Now, when a child is being made in the womb of the mother it is of course the result of the mixing of certain cellular tissue of its two parents, and the one who has the most material of force or energy of psychic matter is the one who supplies the sex organs.

Thus, if a man is very full of what is known as sex-impulse the child will be a boy, and if the woman has the sex-impulse strongest at the time the child will be a girl. You cannot control this instinct, it is not entirely physical, but partly psychic, as it is rarely within the decision of the entirely human factors to say whether a child shall be male or female. The deciding factor is what particular type of soul is waiting to be born into that particular family, for every child born has its own particular niche in the world which no one else can fill, whether the destiny is to be great or humble.

Sex is not at all what your own people think it ; it is very wonderful really, not low or bestial, nor a means of gratifying sensations. It is a law occult and most interesting, because it is really part of a great Cosmic Idea.

Know then, that whenever man or woman sell their bodies for material gain, for lust, or for any wrongful purpose, their sin is hateful in the sight of God, Whose laws are absolutely pure in every manner of manifestation.

We are all part of a stupendous scheme of evolution, evolving on laws not even glimpsed by your scientific men. All parts are dependent on each other, even in many petty ways not even thought of by your people.

When the sex of the child is decided, and this is on the day when the cellular tissues flow together, the Guides of the Soul which is going to be born are ordered to take charge of this seed as it becomes active in taking shape. The etheric body begins to make itself into form, then the child suddenly becomes alive in the body of the mother, and one day the child ripens like a perfect fruit and in due course is born with the amulet necklace of its past lives in its auric surround. The etheric body is much larger than the physical as it is a part of a wider world of dimensions.

Q. Is the aura part of the astral body ? Both seem to be coloured.

A. Not at all. The aura is really the picture of the development of the spiritual character. It is a very important part of the human make-up. It is most sensitive and very easily put wrong by noise, or distasteful surroundings. Whereas the etheric body tells the condition of health and the general mental conditions, the aura reflects all the highest qualities of the spiritual knowledge, and the highest aspirations of the soul.

Q. Does the baby bring its aura with it ?

A. Not when it is first born. It brings a kind of auric matter surrounding it, but it does not develop until the child's own spiritual character begins to develop, which may not make the slightest attempt for a few years. The aura may of course be beautiful or it may be full of ugliness and bad lights. It may be that of a very young uncontrolled soul, it may be that of a saint.

Q. What then is the astral body ?

A. Your astral body is the body of your desire emotions ; a kind of addition to your etheric body, developing side by side with it, not at all independent of the soul, but the more material part of it, as a soul is all part of the whole constitution of man as we know him.

Q. Can a clairvoyant discriminate between the astral body, the etheric body, and the aura ?

A. Not always. That is why accounts are conflicting about what is seen in the colours which surround a person.

Everything has its etheric counterpart because its form was first part of the ether of mental conceptions, and though many things have astral bodies, they will never get spiritual bodies.

CHAPTER XIII

THE CONSTITUTION OF MAN (*contd.*)

(b) *The Human Body*

The Mental Body. The Pineal Gland. The Pituitary Gland. Mind and Matter. Spinal Column. Law of Rhythm. The Human Battery. The Magnetic Body. Blood. The Heart and Hands. The Etheric Body. Solar Plexus. Spleen. The Physical Body. Genital and Excretory Organs. The Four Triangles.

THE HUMAN BODY.

There are four chief centres in the human body. These centres correspond to the four bodies of which we wish to talk, for although the MAN consists of the great triad of body and soul and spirit, he also has varying degrees of sheaths (for want of a better word), so that each part of him is interwoven with the other, and on the dense physical body you will find the visible organs of subtle or invisible bodies.

THE MENTAL BODY.

Now let us first consider the head, which is of course the seat of all the best and highest faculties, controlling, as it undoubtedly does, the whole of man's external make-up ; the Headquarters, as we may very truly call it, for in the head is to be found the real connecting link with the higher aspects of manifestation, namely, the gland known to your mind as the pineal gland, about which very little is really understood : for this gland is the casket of essences peculiarly adapted to be used for contacting the unseen forces ; it is the receiving station of all psychic power of the higher kind, the rudimentary all-seeing eye, as it were, for without a well-developed gland, the man remains very much engulfed in the ordinary routine of material life.

We can always see at a glance the rate at which a person's development is proceeding by the rate at which this gland vibrates. It is very closely connected with your own physical brain, but yet something quite apart from it in function, for the brain is a kind of warehouse of sensations, more or less well stored and regulated, whereas the pineal gland is an active dynamo, full of potential life and creative force. This gland is very closely connected in function with all creative functions, both mental and physical ; it is the organ which sees ahead, and enables the reincarnating ego to seize the opportunities of carrying out the designs which the soul desires to carry through the particular life ahead of it ; it is really *the brain of the soul*, as it were, so that your mind can understand, it is very necessary to keep it healthy and very sensitive to all good influences, which may impinge upon it from the other planes.

Now, from this pineal gland there is another connection with other planes of consciousness, the pituitary gland, not quite so important, but also very useful and very necessary to understand, for this gland is the very necessary storehouse of sensations answering to the soul's ear ; thus you have each in your own physical bodies the actual physical organs for clairvoyance and clairaudience, making together the instrument for psychic development quite perfect and complete. It is very noteworthy that only of late years your scientists have begun to appreciate the real significance of your body's system of glands, for these have a very occult connection with all that is unseen and all that is unrealized in the outer world of senses.

These senses (or gland centres) were well understood by those who trained the novice for his initiation into the higher consciousness, and all such were taught how to purify these organs of psychic senses in order to contact the unseen forces in Nature, as well as in their own heavenly existences.

These organs were and are very often badly misused in the very dubious paths of black magic ; they were often subjected to horrible forms of ritualistic practices, and made to vibrate to a very quick stimulant known to all magicians who dealt with these evil matters. These drugs gave rise to the terrible visions of the lower astral regions, known later to your own people as the horrors of hell, with terrible fires of devastating yet not destructive or consuming kinds ; devilish forms and hideous, unspeakable entities aroused by the wrong vibration of these sensitive glands, just as when your own wireless is wrongly tuned-in, and your ear is tormented by hideous noise.

These horrors were generally inflicted on the novice during his tests in the earlier stages of initiation ; they were actually personal experiences of each individual, not faked experiences ; and only by serenity in trial and a very firm hold of the higher senses could a man escape with his sanity, restored to his own personal comfort, as your ritual remarks.

How little your minds really know ! To this day these experiences are yours in your own[1] ritual practices, when undertaken in earnest, particularly when occultism is directly invoked. Never, never admit these into your own midst, but during the stages of darkness preserve a very real attitude of prayer for guidance in all the intricate pathways of the soul's adventure, for even in your own Lodges this soul's adventure is a very real undertaking.

Now let us continue with our remarks on the psychic instrument within your own body. These two glands have always been the real secret places of the Most High in every human body, and by earnest prayer and meditation their powers may be very greatly increased. Meditation during which special attention is focused with knowledge on these glands is very important. All stimulating alcoholic drinks are of course false aids and often very dangerous aids to this kind of exercise. This was originally the use of wine in religious rites ; it produced a state of coma or so-called ecstasy, or divine intoxication, very useful it is true, but very dangerous, as its abuse led to the present vice of drunkenness.

When your brains have understood these two glands and their uses in your physical heads, your next step is to try to grasp the effect their uses have on your whole body. When your people talk of the victory of mind over matter, they really are very glibly talking of a fact they do not rightly understand, for the truth is, that the real victory over matter, or over your physical bodies, is by the right and harmonious reception of the great healing and har-

[1] i.e. Masonic.

monious vibrations playing on the battery in your own headquarters, from our own inner or higher power-station, whence all healing and health of mind and body proceed.

This is really at the back of so-called Christian Science, but the exponents do not rightly use those powers, because they mistrust all psychic development. This is foolish, and deprives them of much power that might be theirs ; their attitude is one of denial ; it is wrong ; it should be one of recognition of inharmony as a definite ill, and of a sympathetic working on the lines of directing definite currents of harmonious force to play on the sufferer.

Now, when these forces are properly directed with prayer, concentration, the laying on of hands, there is a very great deal of sickness and suffering which may be healed at once ; but the body being an independent collection of all sorts of inhabitants, as it were, in the nerve cells, the muscles and in the blood, it is just as well to know something about the other great centres in the body, which play such important parts in the happy, healthful being called Man. For Man was meant to be happy, and it should be the aim of every one to be, and to seek and make happiness all around him.

The very important part of the human structure is of course the spinal column, the seat of so much nerve force and of nervous troubles. Your battery sends special connecting wires down into your spine, and if those wires are tampered with, either by accident or by folly, then the whole body lacks the perfect harmony of perfect health.

If your spines are strong and justly balanced, your whole physical system is at once in proper adjustment for the very harmonious working-out of your own system in the microcosm ; for so is man placed on his own axis, from his own centre, that is really his own special centre or point within the universe. He is also related to the greater force which your minds call God, Who is the centre of your own particular universe, too, so that, systems within systems, all are very closely bound together, linked-up, as it were, into one splendid and perfect pattern, or one vast cosmic design of perfection.

Your spinal column is not very well understood in your world, though the newer forms of osteopathy are really looking into this matter far more intelligently than so far has been the custom. All children should have their spines properly and most scientifically examined during their years of growth, so little can set them just out of the perfect line, and so much suffering may be avoided by just this little precaution in early years.

Q. Why are so many human spines crooked when it is so important that they should be straight ?

A. Because your human bodies are not so very well-proportioned as they ought to be. This is due to many causes ; the extravagances of your modern civilization is one cause ; the unnatural method of educating small children by making them remain over books and such-like for long periods of time before the spine is properly set ; the method of wrong feeding. Your savage seldom errs in this respect, his body is often in advance of his white and civilized brother because his life is wild and free from all physical restrictions when he is a child.

Q. What happens to the etheric counterpart when the physical model has been made from it ?

A. Your etheric counterpart becomes part of your physical model, it is the etheric body, the mental concept exists still and is enmeshed or rather surrounds the physical model.

When the spine is straight, the connection between the head battery, ourselves and your own earth forces is well prepared for a more harmonious manner of development, and there is no reason at all why, under these good conditions, the whole human frame should not respond to all the great and wonderful rhythmic forces around your earth plane, through it, and in every dimension too ; for remember, the whole purpose of life is to establish rhythm.

Your minds ask why bother about Nature Forces ? What have they to do with your personal lives on your present earth plane ? That is where your puny intellects fail so often. Your object or goal lies far ahead of your present lives on earth. Can your minds not yet understand the tremendous and inspiring beauty of an immanence of Godhood (if one may use such a term) in all that is seen, felt, realized ; in all the sights, sounds, and emotions of everyday life ? How much more then should your hearts not seek the hidden wisdom and beauty of what as yet is hidden from your human eyes, ears, and understandings ?

Seek Nature's heart, and she will fill your souls with unspeakable raptures, such as will wipe away all tears, all vain regrets, all sorrows, pettinesses, and then turn from Nature unto Nature's Master, unto her Father and yours.

We spoke some time ago of the law of rhythm[1] ; it is a law on which depends the perfect poise of the bodies in all planes of matter. Your own Greek teachers were wise in their generation, they knew the value of healthy, perfect bodies, and when a candidate presented himself for their mystery schools, they demanded perfect health of him, or he would not be able to respond to the play of psychic forces of his mental battery. As soon as licentious or gross-living men began to be admitted, then the power of their schools began to be overthrown.

Your bodies to be really useful must first be healthy, that is why your present interest in child-welfare is being stimulated in your world to-day. Work very hard to establish this higher rate of health vibrations amongst your people. We know it will help on the spiritual evolution of the world. Start with the infant and much will develop in the races to come.

Let us try to give a clear understanding of rhythm, as it is very important. Now try to realize that all life starts from its own centre. This centre is the point of contact with the oversoul, or to carry it back even further, the point of contact with God. But as God is a Spirit (to quote your own Scriptures), then the great oversoul is God-in-essence. Now this point of contact to the human body is the battery in the head, and from that battery the axis or spinal column projects, and to this axis belongs the function of regulating the individual life of peaceful and harmonious existence.

Your minds are accustomed to think of yourselves from your feet upwards. So long as your feet are planted on the earth, your spine on the frame of the trunk, and your heads on the top, then your minds can think of man's stability. But in reality, your minds should think of your spine depending from the junction of this battery (positive and negative) and the rest of your body merely depending, or being connected up with this axis from this centre. We do not regard you as persons walking upright on a solid earth,

[1] See p. 29.

H

we regard your central pivot apart from your so-called solid earth ; we see your batteries spark, as it were, in a surrounding plane of subtle matter (which we will call the surrounding, penetrating ether of space) and your spines stick out like so many infinitesimal rods or needles, with appendages, which you call limbs and so forth. You can now perhaps understand the reason for our not always being accurate in our prognostications of earth plane events, they often do not appear to us here unless they leave a very distinct mark on the surrounding auras.

Now the human body with its centre, its axis, and its own special pathway in the system of evolution has a movement between two poles,[1] and these movements, if truly and perfectly rhythmic, wing to and fro, in perfect harmony, like a properly set pendulum of a clock. Remember here that the rhythmic swing of a clock's pendulum always being a slow, regular, and never ceasing progress, a clock, whose pendulum is working, never remains at the same time ; it moves on with proper gradation of that which your minds must regard as a type of progression, never of retrogression, or of standstill.

Now your mind is very uneasy about this mechanical idea, but it is not so difficult if your brain for one moment will think of your own body as something which is made up of a very wonderous system of bright and beautiful creatures called cells working in harmony, and making up in their entirety the overseer or head-being, which your mind knows as the personality ; then you can see that we see far more than this sparking point and its needle ; we see the wondrous collection of subtle and very beautiful cells, or multiple lives, which we know as *YOU*, the ego, the being called by the name which is yours for the time being ; but we talk from a very much higher standpoint than is usually spoken about, because we are trying to teach you something of your own Cosmic life and your very close connection with the life of the universe.

Already it has become possible for your brains to regard your physical bodies from a very different aspect, so now let us consider a very interesting point about the spinal column.

Now this spinal column is, as we remarked, a kind of needle or connecting rod, with the head battery formed of

[1] i.e. The Oversoul and the Earth-plane. See diagram, p. 119.

the two glands, and when acting in proper concert, this forms the real point of attraction between our own higher spheres and your own earthly bodies. It is very difficult, of course, for your minds or rather your brains to follow this rather unusual point of regard, yet it is very necessary to follow it out carefully, in order to understand the healing art and many of the so-called magical practices common among occultists[1] of all descriptions.

THE MAGNETIC BODY.

The magnetic body is the body of the emotions ; the etheric body the body of the etheric, the breathing part of the physical body ; the soul is the fourth-dimensional body, the spiritual above, beyond, and transcending all these. It will make matters clear if you make a diagram ; we will try to help your pencil with it.

The magnetic body has as its main organ the heart ; that is why your minds speak of heart-ache, of sorrow of the heart, and such-like ; it is perfectly correct ; here again the subtle, unseen, magnetic body has its visible and outer organ—the heart and its necessary fluid, the blood.

The emotions rule a man's life more openly than any other apparently ; we say apparently because, of course, man is ruled from a more secret set of functioning ideas, but the ordinary man's response is through his emotions, and as he appeals to the emotions of his fellow beings, so will his influence be great or insignificant for good or for evil. The heart represents fire and the blood supplies that warmth which keeps the physical body warmed and in good condition.

[1] Your friends are not very happy about this word ; it connotes to them the less pleasant arts of the unknown, and therefore feared experiences of the inner planes. But tell them they need not be anxious, for we never allow those who seek knowledge for the highest uses to be badly or dangerously treated.

Evils exist on almost all the lower planes, physical, astral, mental, and vary in kind according to the special plane on which the soul is at the moment functioning. The most obvious are the dense physical ones of the senses, then the emotional and then the subtler ones of the mental, subtle and very insidious, because the line of demarcation is at times not clearly defined.

Pride, love of power, lawful ambitions, and so forth all may be justifiable to a very limited extent, but their limit is very easily passed.

You talk of blood heat : it is the useful healthy temperature of food, etc.

All complaints of the blood retard the efficiency of a healthy body ; a fever burns it up. Anger, love, bitterness, all these emotions of heat and cold are part of the great magnetic essence of your whole planetary system, of which the sun is the outer symbol in your own world's system. The magnetic power of your sun is the ruling planet of your earth, your world could not exist without it ; it governs races, so that those races whose lives are lived in hot countries are quite different from those living in cold or less sun-influenced lands.

The hands are two of the minor adjuncts or aids to the heart ; the hands give, heal, destroy, fondle ; they are true symbols of a man's character.

THE ETHERIC BODY.

Now let us tell your mind about the etheric body, for this too is very important ; it has two organs in your physical body, the solar-plexus and the spleen. These are the rulers of the nervous system, and of great use in the development of the psychic faculties.

The occultist learns early the use of the solar-plexus, and the manifesting medium uses the spleen from which issues the material known in your world as ectoplasm ; it is really generated by the combined action of these two organs.

Here, again, a man must learn control of his nervous system, or he will make no real soul progress, but will be a prey and an easy one to the undesirable manifesting entities of the unseen forces who hover between your own world and the world immediately beyond. We use this word because it is difficult not to use a word which really gives that dimension or place, it is not really apart, it also interpenetrates.

THE PHYSICAL BODY.

The lower part of the human frame is typical of the physical body as a purely physical creation. It contains the generating organs, the excretory organs, and the legs

and feet which keep a man attached to the dense physical
body of your own earth plane.

The genitals are the visible organs of this body, specially
connected with the higher or unseen forces, one in a man,
one in a woman, uniting to create fresh life, the most abused,
although the most divine parts of the human body, because
in this dense and earthy body lies the supreme power of
reproducing life which may become very God of very God.

Q. It does not seem by this method that the etheric
body has any connection with the ether, the ether of space,
the dodecahedron of the Greeks.

A. No, there is no real connection at all. The etheric
body is really part of the subtler emanations of your own
body. Ether of space is a term not really understood at
present ; it is a dimension into which only the more highly
evolved man-spirit can function ; it is reality ; whereas
your earth conditions are transitory and therefore not
reality. The symbol of the dodecahedron is a symbol of
the perfected soul or archetypal man. Real man, not little
one-sided man ; the perfected being, who has passed
through all phases of earthly experience, gone far on into
other planes, and become an inhabitant of another branch
of superman's evolution. The only connection in actual
terms of speech is in the fact that the physical sheath being
forever laid aside, the densest body of this being is etheric
or subtle. Etheric as applied to the still human frame is
merely a subtle emanation, perhaps we might call it the
rudimentary body of a higher being.

Your brain has worked our information out in the four
squares.[1] Do you not see that the square is a type of man,
also the pyramid ? Now see how the other ideas of the
number seven became part of the whole, for there are three
aspects on each plane of existences : Spirit or life (that is,
vibration), substance, and form ; that which initiates ;
that which conceives ; that which is produced—the universal trinity.

Now let us go on with this diagram. The lungs are
part of your magnetic body, but also the connecting link
with the upper or mental part too.

---

[1] See diagram p. 120.

Now consider for a moment the real functions of the separate parts of your outward body as a big whole.

Your breath is the first substance which brings life into your mould form, or body. The child *is* not, until it is separated from its mother ; that is, when, by the separation of the cord, it breathes independently.

Next let us consider the nervous system, the very sensitive part of your body, which is really the body which is dependent on the senses, even though their uses are directed by the battery in the brain part of your whole organization. The nerves are, of course, aided (even, one might say, expressed) in a physical manner through the power of your muscles ; whilst actual dense form is entirely due to the proper functioning of the etheric and the physical bodies through the proper and healthy functions of the food organs, the gland system, and all the provisions made to store, use, and dismiss food substances and creative substances.

Your diagram explains how the human creature is between two poles, the oversoul and the physical earth plane, with the spine forming the axis ; so the human being revolves on its own axis in a system of human evolution. Just so the earth revolves on its own axis in its own journey or evolution in its own planetary system.

Hence the axiom that man the microcosmos is the miniature copy of the great macrocosmos.

Man = the square, i.e. with his four bodies, physical, etheric, magnetic, and mental.

Start with your mental triangle on your diagram and we have the first outpouring of spirit essence, into a form by means of a material which we will call energy or electricity, the spark, i.e. produced by the clashing of the two forces.

Energy, attraction, the vital spark.

In the magnetic triangle the substance is astral (in varying degrees of density), the spirit is as your mind sees colour-vibration, and the form is the mould of the man's astral body or aura.

In the etheric body the substance is etheric, electric in spirit, luminous in form.

The physical is animal in form, flesh in substance, spiritually divine.

DIAGRAM I

Man and his bodies between oversoul and earth, showing the physical centres.

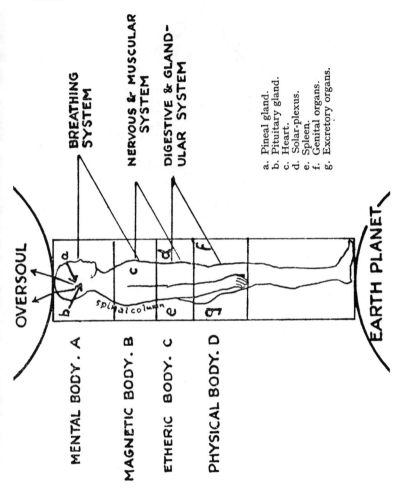

DIAGRAM II

Man shown as a pyramid in the flat or net.

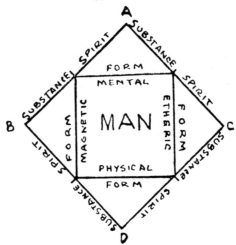

Spirit.	Substance	Form.
A. Energy	Spirit essence	Vital spark.
B. Colour vibration	Astral	Astral body or Aura.
C. Electric	Etheric	Luminous or Health Aura.
D. Divine	Flesh	Animal (i.e. man).

CHAPTER XIV

THE CONSTITUTION OF MAN (*contd.*)

(c) *The Soul*

Soul Material. Nirvana. Harmony with Nature. The Great Soul
and the Lesser Soul. Soul Form. The Oversoul. Adam and Eve.
The Fall. The Two Lost Senses. The Soul's Progress. Discipleship.
Spirit Names.

SOUL MATERIAL.

Know then, that the soul is formed of a very subtle kind
of matter which has its origin in the higher mental spheres.
Nothing at all of what your mankind terms the astral plane
has any connection with this body called the soul. This
is where so many teachings are inaccurate, for they mistake
what is a kind of emanation from the etheric matter for
what is far more spiritual and subtle, that is this matter
which (for want of a word suitable to express it) we must
call the mind-body or soul-body.

Now, this body is a very beautiful body of essence which
is very part of the great oversoul, the *anemos* of the Greeks,
the fluid part of organic life ; that is, that which is in all life
throughout your universe.

For soul is a part of all cosmic and all eternal life force ;
the gross material is not really life as we understand it, for
material life is most transitory and constantly changing
its form, whereas soul is something permanent or relatively
so, for it persists as soul-essence in all ages, and is only
changed from a less subtle variety into a most glorious and
very fine or subtle variety.

When a soul is struck off, or sent out from the great
universal mass of soul-material, it takes on a form which
it retains until it becomes so worked up into perfection,
that it is ready to be absorbed into the all glorious and

Cosmic body of the oversoul, but that is a process demanding unimaginable periods of countless ages and not within the human consciousness at all.

Here your mind sees the origin of the Brahman idea of Nirvana. It is beyond human desire and certainly beyond human understanding.

Let us consider soul bodies as they more readily may be understood by your own limited consciousness, for we, too, are very far from that final glory ; it remains the great incomprehensible to us here, but we know of it as a so-called final state of truth, the back of reality, the I AM of the entire Universal Cosmos, the completed universal of all systems of universes.

This is enough for any mind to grasp for the present, so do not waste time attempting to grope beyond your own special universe.

Now, the individualized particle which we call the human soul is, as we remarked before, a veritable part of the over-soul, and this oversoul permeates all nature (that is, all natural phenomena) as sensed by your own very limited senses, and of course all the unseen part, too, as seen by us over here.

The Great Nature Spirits, or Devas, are the unseen soul forces, too, and play their own special part in this vast scheme of life manifestation. It is very possible for one of your own kind to be so " tuned-in " to the vibration of the great Spirits, that there is a kind of sympathetic under-standing between their souls and yours. They are very powerful Beings, and are very resistless in their working out of their schemes, and when Masters wish to train their disciples for work on higher planes of consciousness, they advise their disciples to seek intercourse with these beautiful Beings, for they know that there is a very close kinship with the souls of men and the souls of Nature-Spirit Masters or Devas.

In the hearts of all true lovers of Nature there is a seed or line (perhaps this is the better expression) of communication set between Man and Nature, for remember Man is not only related to God, he is related to the Universe, that is, to the particular plane of materialization on which his earth-body lives, moves, suffers, and learns.

As man learns to be in harmony with Nature, to love her,

to draw into himself the exquisite treasures of her divine breath, so Nature will reveal herself more and more to his delighted senses ; and we mean purified, loving senses, nothing sensual or luxuriously sensuous, but a lifting-up of the ordinary senses into a fine rapture of love, understanding, and enjoyment of beauty in essence, beauty materialized into outward forms, colours, perfume, sounds, and ecstasies.

This is one of the many joys awaiting the true lover of immortal beauty.

Now, when this very simple state of realization has been sensed or touched, it will be understood that just as man's soul is linked up with the Great Soul of Nature, so, too, the man's soul must be linked up with other forces unseen, unrealized, and yet all-pervading, the great oversoul of man's own evolution. This will not be so easy to follow because there is really no outward form as is the case in Nature. The sole means of coming into contact here, until a highly developed psychic development is attained, is entirely through intuition, which is, of course, a very strongly developed sense in some of your people ; but none may enter into the close communion enjoyed by the few, until a very closely tried allegiance has been established between your souls and the souls of others and the souls of your special Guides over here.

You wondered if your soul-bodies were altogether attached, or only partly so, to your earthly bodies. They are only partly attached, and only a very small part at that, so that when a person appears to live very much in the clouds, as your tongues express it, they are very often not at all in their bodies, but living in other planes of matter. Very trying at times, your people will say. Yes, that is perfectly true, but make the best of them, they may be living lives of wonderful experience entirely unknown to their physical brains. The soul life is a life apart ; the older or more experienced the soul, the more busy the life of the soul. They take back to your earth the gifts of inspirational powers, they will be pioneers ; many will inaugurate movements, yet fail in the detail of carrying out, but that will be done by others, whose souls are more closely linked to their bodies on earth.

These soul-bodies have form, though not quite using the word as your people use it. Form to your people denotes physical organs ; and though in a measure your physical organs are reproductions of patterns inaugurated in the great school of mind production here, the forms which your souls have are recognizable as forms even in your sense of this term, but forms without the limits set in the grosser fleshly bodies. They are of a wonderful opaque luminosity of colour, which is best realized in what your minds would understand as the auras of each person, and this luminosity depends for intensity and brilliance upon the special age or development of your souls.

Let us give you an example which may help your brains to realize this idea. Your bodies are composed of millions of cells, muscles, nerves, all kinds of organisms, over which you yourselves (that is, your so-called intelligences) have neither power, knowledge, nor control ; yet each cell, muscle, and nerve leads its own life quite independently of your intelligence, and your intelligence leads its life quite apart from cell-life, nerve-life, and so on. Your intelligence cannot deny the life of these cells and so forth, because science has revealed their existence and their functions. Your nerves and so forth do not concern themselves with your intelligences, yet your whole material body is inextricably bound up in the existence of intelligence, cells, nerves, muscles, and so on. In a measure this is what is happening to your soul-body—it is aware of your physical body and its life ; it even works with it and through it ; but your physical body is only dimly aware of this soul-body, and works on without paying much heed to it.

Now, this soul-body, which, as your brain knows already is a very definite body, is that part of your own microcosm which is linked up with the vast organism known as the OVERSOUL. This oversoul is the Soul of the Universe, and this, in its turn, is a part of the Great and Universal Logos, or OVERSOUL OF THE UNIVERSES, these universes existing in incalculable numbers as the manifested parts of GOD.

Each soul was originally separated into fragments struck off from this great SOUL MASS, which is primordial, and above all human conception in essence, and each fragment was sent into denser material, not fleshly bodies at this point but subtle soul-bodies. Then came the division into two parts again, whilst still in these subtler bodies. The story given as the creation of Adam and Eve, remember, happened before humanity (as your minds now know it) existed on the earth at all. The so-called Garden of Eden was never on this earth plane of yours at all ; it was in the mental sphere or plane, and man fell into material bodies already created into moulds or forms, but not originally intended for these soul-bodies at all. This was the period of the actual Fall.[1] It was at this point that these soul-bodies began to separate themselves from one another, and though there were equal divisions of male or positive souls, and female or receptive (that is negative) souls, the outer physical bodies were not strictly male for male souls, and female for female souls, but the souls became enmeshed or condensed into material bodies in which certain experiences had to be worked out.

Experience to be gained is always the deciding factor when a soul-body seeks reincarnation on your plane.

Now, this soul-essence, being involved in a so-called man-body, began its individual life with very great limitations in one respect, and not always under very good conditions, for affinities were separated at an early date, and there began the idea of separation.

It was, however, only the human envelope which was the dividing body, since there is no separation in the OVER-SOUL, all is complete harmony and union, but the small fragment which became enmeshed in the fleshly body became oblivious of any part of itself which it could not sense with the organs known as the five senses, though at first they were conscious of seven.

As the ages passed two of these senses became submerged, and your ordinary man speaks of seven senses yet recognises only five.

Where are these two lost senses ? That is a question

---

[1] Q. Can you explain the Fall ?

A. The Fall was not a fall into the earth plane at all, but a descent from the spiritual plane into the mental planes. These planes were in existence in the Cosmic system many æons before the earth became habitable to mankind. When these spiritual entities were condemned to fall into denser bodies they suffered great loss of spiritual energy, and by energy we must understand powers of knowledge. This made it more possible for forces which were not really spiritual, but occult or magical, to attract these entities yet lower still, and so they fell into denser astral bodies.

Here their development was arrested for a very long period of time until by degrees the astral regions were invaded by certain beings, mankind in a lower degree of development and fusion became possible.

The Sons of God were one with the daughters of Men.

often asked. Yes, that is the real tragedy of the human fall—the loss of those two senses, for they were the actual senses contacting man's greater soul-body, and when man lost cognizance of them, he lost ordinary touch with that part of his constitution—the great soul-body, and knew, even then, not very certainly of his smaller soul-body.

Q. My little soul is sitting here in my material body taking down this writing—what is my big soul doing?

A. Your big soul is also writing, for at this moment your soul-body is in harmony with us on these higher planes, and we are discussing matters of vast importance, nothing less than the constitution of man the immortal soul.

Q. But this self at this moment is only really conscious, i.e. personally conscious, of the little soul in this indifferent fleshly body, just taking down automatically what a band of unseen, physically unknown spirit entities choose to write through me.

A. Yes, that is true, but a little more practice will reveal what is known by your great soul to your little fragment of a soul, and to your outer human consciousness. In sleep there is no division at all, your soul is a great and very beautiful form, your physical eyes would not recognize it.

Q. But when I go about my ordinary everyday life of ordering, mending clothes, paying bills or calls, what is my big soul doing?

A. Your big soul is very busy carrying on its work of learning how to render our mystical teaching of practical value to the world in general.

Your soul never ceases to work for this, that is why we are able to get into contact at once with your earthly body ; it is not at all that we are at your beck and call, but that your soul is in constant attendance at our own school of mystical instruction, and when your physical body sits down to receive our words, or vibrations which result in words, your mind conveys what is really continually going on in the education of your soul under our special tutelage.

Q. Does the same bit of soul constantly reincarnate?

A. Why describe it as a bit? There is no separateness into pigeon-holes, that is peculiar to the human mind ; your soul is a big beautiful form and a part of it functions in a body ; just as your hand is put into a glove, but is still part of your naked body. The glove serves to protect it from wind, or sun, or brambles, yet it is still part of the beautiful naked body made in a wonderful mould.

Q. There are many who do not work for psychic ends, many who are leading rather rotten lives, giving way to drink and all kinds of stupid things, others leading entirely empty lives ; what is the big soul doing in this case ? Is this also beautiful beyond recognition and so forth ?

A. In such cases the soul is at a standstill, and makes no progress at all. One day the progress will have to start, but meanwhile these souls are asleep in a kind of stupor state ; these unfortunate people are in effect asleep, and impervious to all the great advancement of which they might be an active influence. That is why teaching and preaching are so necessary for humanity. Often a slumbering soul is roused into activity by the words of a book or a sermon, or by the action of a friend on this side or on your own, and the soul begins a new life.

Now let us tell you that this soul life is very important, because it decides the number of incarnations, for the total number of incarnations varies and is decided by the manner in which each test or life is passed, and the state of psychic development achieved in each life.

Yes, as your brain remarked, some pyschic people are " perfect rotters " ; that is very true, but their experiences may be best finished in other planes of existence or even on other planets, though, as a rule, there is very little inter-planetary intercourse, the lines of evolution being quite different.

Do not regard incarnation on your earth plane as an evil. It was not intended to be only a place of certain limits for a short period of time ; this is often a very happy period, and always a period of immense advantage to the aspiring soul. As the soul expands and feels these limitations less, these advantages outweigh the sufferings so often experienced.

Let each person work for the advancement of the earth plane, and in time there will be far less misery, and much more happiness. Meanwhile the souls of the righteous are in the hands of God, and there shall no evil touch them. Evil is illusory, transitory ; true joy endureth for ever, in the Kingdom of God, which is in the realms of the souls of those whose work is well and truly done.

It is now time that we told you about the new life which starts whenever a soul steps out of the mass into the higher planes of development, for when the soul takes this step there is as a rule no turning back, or if the soul turns back, its punishment, self-inflicted, is terrible. That is the outer darkness referred to by the Master Jesus, the outer darkness of the lower astral kingdoms ; for the soul, having once assumed certain spiritual responsibilities, is expected to go forward, gaining wisdom and understanding, to be filled with all the gifts of the spirit ; but once having gone back on this great step, the experience is terribly unhappy and evil.

Such is the lot of all who dabble unwisely or wickedly with occult wisdom ; such will be the experience of all dabblers in magic of the perverted kind ; all moral perverts, all blasphemers, all those whose awakened souls, having once seen the true light, have turned towards the darkness.

Those whose souls have not developed yet are not exposed to these terrors of darkness ; theirs is merely the darkness of ignorance, and many lives will work through these states ; it is only the wilfully evil that suffer in this terrible way. Those who suffer perverted instincts will suffer greatly in their future lives in other planes and in their future incarnations.

There is a very strange point with regard to sex perversion ; it is this—that real perversion is the result of very uncontrolled sexual habits in past incarnations, and if these habits persist there comes one day a terrible annihilation of those whose immortal souls are smirched with this grave sin.

But the soul which steadfastly turns towards the light, is soon helped by those whose vibrations are able to be contacted. The soul becomes aware of its Angel Guide and helpers, and in due course it is definitely taken in hand, trained, tested, and given such initiations as it may be capable of passing. Later in its experience it is able to become aware of its real greatness ; the " little bit " is rendered completely aware of its big soul, and enlightenment is accomplished.

The giving of a spirit name is a very great advance on the path, the gift of discipleship follows almost at once, and when once the soul is accepted as a disciple, there is joy in the Kingdom of Heaven, as your Master Jesus said, over him that turneth Homeward. The prodigal son is received into His Father's House. Here there is no returning to the lower life of the senses : the soul has caught a glimpse of reality, and all other things are small in comparison to this wonderful recovery of the lost sonship. From this point the growth of the soul in the hidden gifts is very speedy, and in due course the soul leaves the earth plane never to return unless for special work.

Q. In the case of a baby whose soul is already that of a disciple, what is happening to the big soul while the baby is growing to full consciousness ?

A. The tiny baby is only a speck of the real being who is being incarnated for another life for a special purpose. The soul is still at work in the higher planes, his tiny body is hardly part of it yet ; his soul-fragment is not completely enmeshed in his body, but in due course it will take full possession. Meanwhile his body is being specially guarded by his guides as the casket prepared for his soul's use in the near future.

CHAPTER XV

THE CONSTITUTION OF MAN (*contd.*)

(d) *The Evolution of the Soul*

The Sons of God. The Younger Souls. Birth-control.

Q. WE are still in the dark as to the origin of the soul of those who are designated as younger or unevolved souls ?

A. This point represents difficulty to you because your finite minds make a distinction between the soul-essence and the oversoul, they are interchangeable terms. When the first great and individualized souls were sent forth, to fall eventually into human moulds, they were evolved up to a very high degree but lacked certain experience which their immersion in physical form was to give them ; they " fell," as the words are given you in your various scriptures, and became fragments of divine essence which were to struggle through many incarnations until they had gained freedom of fleshly fetters by freedom of will ; that was a great achievement.

Now those whom your minds regard as younger or less evolved souls do not belong to this category at all ; they are separate fragments of a later outpouring, not being enmeshed in physical bodies until physical bodies were in a much further state of development. The divine souls were pioneers, the younger souls were portions of the less individualized soul-essence, that is, the essence which is universally spread about in the realms of the oversoul.

Q. Are those first pioneers the " Sons of God ? "

A. Yes, that is, they were individualized within higher realms of the spirit and were sent down to help humanity.

Now the question of the soul's evolution is a very necessary point to understand, for it is a point on which there is much ignorance amongst ordinary people, and in the Christian teaching this ignorance is especially noteworthy, and your Christian preachers and teachers are entirely unable to teach or preach aright.

Know then, my children, that the first souls of all were those radiant souls which emanated from the Father in the very beginning (and by the Father we mean your special Heavenly Father), and He it is Whose love will welcome back yourselves, His own prodigal sons, into the heavenly mansions of which your Great Master Jesus spoke.

Now these souls, emanating from the Great Father-Mother GOD (to give your Heavenly Progenitor the full title) were first sent forth as divine sons of one body, yet combining the double aspect of male and female. These were in existence on the highest spiritual planes, many æons before real form-life started on your special earth planet.

As these souls spread over wider areas of existence, they were, in due course, divided into two aspects, but still on a very exalted degree of consciousness, and still in most etherealized bodies.

Now there were certain ruling spirits amongst the radiant soul entities who sought to become rulers among these souls, and by reason of a wrongful ambition, they were drawn into denser and less etherealized bodies, so that they lost the brightest and highest aspect of their heritage.

In time they fell yet further into denser bodies, not even yet physical ones, and a certain number were sent as rulers and spiritual leaders to help on the evolution of certain beings, allied to your human race, on a land which was long before the Atlantean civilization ; but much evil was in this race, it was destroyed ultimately, and a new one was formed in the continent known as Atlantis.

Here these special souls were drawn into real physical bodies by force of attraction ; it was not exactly an evil thing, but, by so doing, they lost the highest aspect of their soul's heritage, and by degrees became entirely immersed into human families, but they remain the leaders and pioneers of all the best types of progress, and were the salvation of those who were the finest of the Atlantean races.

When through bad occult practices the greater part of this civilization was swept away in a vast series of cataclysms, these original souls were incarnated into the leaders of the newer Aryan races, and in your own midst to-day there are a certain number of initiates who still linger on your earth to help humanity. It is their own special form of service.

Now try to remember that these souls are of direct divine descent, and that their experience has continued through very many lives, not only on your own earth, but on many other planets as well, but planets not known to your own astronomers.

Now let us return to the souls of less high origin. We have already told your mind of the existence of soul-essence, or soul-material—the great oversoul, which is a cosmic essence, and used by the beings called gods to infuse into moulds or forms. This happens on other schemes of systems, but we will deal only with your earth planet.

Now this material was cast forth from the Great I AM, and is the sacred fire or breath which was used to breathe into certain forms, so that they became living souls, as your own scriptures tell you. This essence is of the I AM and is Divine, but it is amazingly difficult to give this to your mind because we are forced to use terms quite incorrect in meaning and in implication, yet are there no other means of conveying these truths.

Try to imagine a vast and very tenuous cloud of living fire, and try to understand that every spark of that cloud of fire has the potentialities of Godhood, and, therefore, that each spark may (when duly breathed into a form) become so vital to that form, that the form cannot exist without it, and that its vitality is so great that it transmutes that whole inert mass of physical atoms into a thinking, vibrating, striving, seeking being. Just as a minute portion of yeast alters the body of your loaf of dull dough into a loaf tasty and agreeable, so the speck of divine yeast permeates the dull dough of physical life and renders the human being a partially divinized being.

Through very many incarnations and through personal effort, each speck develops into a finely constituted soul, and in time may look forward to entering the many mansions, just as the original wonderfully individualized soul ; it is only a matter of time.

Now as we have already told you, as time passes on your earth, a great number of souls fulfil their destiny and return no more to earth ; but there is no cessation of evolution, and there is, from time to time, an outpouring of these divine specks of the oversoul into a fresh set of human bodies, and the world's progress is maintained.

But as the world becomes more spiritualized, these later outpourings will become more easily worked up into a quicker degree of development.

Do try to realize that your foolish minds cannot hope to imagine an end so many æons ahead ; work on faithfully your own selves, and leave these vast matters to your own Great and All-Wise Heavenly Father. He knows and adjusts all things, and we wait on His judgment with confidence, knowing that, with all our experience, we, too, are as babes in the vast history of Cosmic and human evolution.

Q. Is birth-control harming evolution by setting limitations ?

A. Nay, foolish ones, this is too insignificant to matter.

Your principles are wrong, because man should control, rather than prevent human birth, in a legitimate way ; but the Great and Heavenly Father will make His own plans to render human bodies possible for the seeking souls to enter. All is in His very safe keeping.

CHAPTER XVI

THE WAY OF ATTAINMENT

(a) *The Quest. Prayer and Meditation. Study.*

Now when a soul is first on the path which leads to final at-one-ment or union, it is conscious of a certain amount of blissful understanding that there is a great individual future before it ; therefore, the mind ceases to complain of the futility and emptiness of life, for life is full, that is, real life is full of a glorious adventure. The divine quest is this adventure, the quest after the hidden treasure, the search after truth, the immense solace of knowing that the present little life is but a short chapter in a vast volume of beauty, wisdom, and understanding.

Man reacts instinctively to happiness ; it is necessary to him, it aids him in his development ; so that when this feeling, that the soul is setting out on a great and glorious adventure, breaks in upon the heart and mind of man, then he arises in spirit and sets his feet firmly upon the path which leads to his Heaven Home.

The soul, at first, encounters many hardships, for straight or narrow is that way, and the broad sunny pathway leading no-whither is always visible to his outer eye, even though his inner vision knows that it is only the illusion of *fata Morgana*—the curse of the desert.

But this path, which leads eventually to the Heaven Home, becomes as time passes full of joyful companionship, for man never really walks alone ; his Guardian Angel, his Spirit Guides, his own familiar friends are constantly with his spirit, and as his eyes become more used to this narrow and uncompromising pathway, he will become more and more aware of these radiant presences.

Every step of the way is watched and guided ; every

sorrow experienced serves its own useful purpose ; and before many years are passed, the man has become aware of very direct evidence of progress, which will allay all doubts in his outer mind or brain-consciousness.

Your brains are not easy to convince ; your intuition must be developed more and more, for the intuition is indeed the mind of a larger soul.

We use these terms—large and small—because your human mind persistently thinks in these degrees, but they are not correct, for there is one soul, as we have already told you, but your brain-consciousness knows only a fragment of this great whole.

There is, of course, much which happens to the soul never known to its brain-consciousness ; often long years are spent in gathering spiritual knowledge, long before the definite point known as the soul's enlightenment arrives, and is recognized as a definite event by that brain-consciousness. We are often on very well-established terms with a soul long before that soul becomes aware of our own presence in its spiritual life at all.

Your souls at this present moment may be learning more than you can convey to the world in general, but this knowledge is only for your own use ; it could never be passed on, for ultimately all soul-experience must be individual, and only by individual striving can this knowledge be attained.

Now there are, of course, methods by which this knowledge becomes definitely attainable. Many methods have been given in various occult and mystical writings and schools. Many are very good and very suitable, but others may be injurious and not on the best lines at all.

The two best points, which will involve much patience and very careful preparation, are those which are recommended by all who seek union with their higher selves, and now your minds really know what *is* meant by the higher self.

These two points are prayer and meditation. They are the only safe means ; posturing may help some, but it may become very mechanical, and very mixed with occult rhythms. These occult rhythms are very good for the more advanced medium or soul, but should not be attempted until the mind, body, and character are in complete harmony with the spiritual demands of the Christ life.

Purity of body, of character, of thoughts, words and deeds, is above all things necessary. That is the first essential; no man or woman should give way to vice of any kind, sensuality, drink, gluttony, cruelty, spitefulness: all such are real deterrents to progress on the spiritual path to God. "If thine eye offend thee, pluck it out, and cast it from thee," such was the very definite instruction given by your Master Jesus. These things are an offence to the Heavenly Father; they form a stumbling block to the soul's progress; they poison the pure stream of the healthful blood in the physical body, for all these things work adversely on the physical system, as your own doctors are now telling your world.

With regard to prayer, regular times and regular prayers are very necessary : in the morning, on awaking, midday— however occupied—and in the night-time before sleeping. The prayers need not be long, they must be coherent and clearly expressed, because a clearly expressed idea is a mental stimulant and fixes the mind and heart very definitely on one point, rather than allowing it to wander vaguely in more or less hazy mists of prayerful thought. The Lord's Prayer is the greatest invocation in your own scriptures, for it is planned on a very great scale of thought. It is very wonderful in its effect if made use of with understanding. Much that is really mystical is contained within what appears to the outer eye as a very simple form of invocation ; but in effect, its appeal is much wider ; much wonderful teaching is written for your guidance did your eyes but discern it. Prayer is indeed dynamic, and if your people were more fully aware of its power they would never fail to pray in reverence and humility ; for prayer is not to be used selfishly, but for the use of spiritual force for the good of others. Make an attempt to pray more often, for your Heavenly Father neither slumbers nor sleeps, and is ever heedful of your calling on His name for all who are in sickness or distress. Prayer is a holding of direct communication with the great spiritual force.

It is also necessary to study at some time in the day a portion of written matter dealing with some special line of thought. This is useful for building the intellect, for intellect forms a most important part of soul progress, since intellect teaches discernment and discrimination.

Meditation is the most important and most difficult part of training the soul, and can only be successfully accomplished after long practice on given lines. Do not confuse concentration with meditation. Concentration may be taught in circles but meditation is a matter of individual striving and cultivation. Concentration is the thought given on a special subject, it is a very good method of holding the thoughts in a very strict method of which much is written in your own books on earth.

When once the mind has decided to follow the lines of individual development, which ends in serious meditation, then a very gradual change takes place in the human body as well as in the soul-body ; all is purified, and all poisonous accumulations in the blood are removed either by some illness, or by a less serious ailment, for these accumulations hinder the actual progress far more than is suspected.

When this has been done, and the physical body cleared, fined, and purified, then it is easy for the first stage of meditation.

It is very soon understood that meditation loosens some link in the chain of physical limitations. Your mind becomes aware of vibrations which are not of the earth plane at all, and your eye, in moments of unawareness, becomes very acutely aware of a change of perspective. Now, when the mind and body are duly prepared by purification, then the whole of the man is ready to follow along the path of psychic development, and it will now be our business to examine these various methods.

CHAPTER XVII

THE WAY OF ATTAINMENT (*contd.*)

(b) Mediumship. Spirit-writing. Time. Names. Method of Testing. Clairvoyance. Clairaudience. Direct Voice. Spirit-photography. Evil Practices.

MEDIUMSHIP.

There are many forms of psychic faculties, and each man has within his aura one of these faculties most clearly indicated. There are many grades in each faculty also, so that a clairvoyant may be able to see spirit-wraiths, or nature-spirits, or if developed on very high lines, then the clairvoyance would be of a most exalted kind, and more or less in actual touch with the inner realms of the higher spiritual planes ; such would see visions of Great Beings, of wonderful places, and yet not in trance at all.

The study of man's various bodies has already given your minds some faint idea of the many grades of emanations, or, in other words, has made your brains acquainted with this vital fact, that all around and all through an ordinary fleshly body there are innumerable dimensions or planes which man is actually able to contact, albeit entirely unknowingly for the most part.

Now it is, of course, evident that as in all cases of development the type of development depends on the level which the soul has reached in its present incarnation, as the different talents whch show forth in his ordinary everyday life are signs, to those that understand, of abilities mental and emotional, which were part of his make-up during his past incarnations.

The many forms of mediumship are due to the particular kind of emanation which is most prevalent for the time being, and a man may be a so-called versatile medium, just as his talents may be of a very varied character.

Sometimes a medium starts as a healer and becomes a great clairvoyant ; sometimes because of being a special kind of clairvoyant the healing faculty follows ; some have the gift of magnetism very strongly developed and become great mediums for materialization, or photography, or for apports. Clairaudience very often precedes spirit or automatic writing, sometimes writing precedes clairaudience. Trance mediumship is very interesting and peculiar to the negative medium, but a positive medium may become momentarily possessed though very seldom goes into a trance ; he stands aside, he does not relinquish entirely.

We will write separately and through another Guide on the subject of healing, but at this moment we will write only of the better known mediumistic qualities of clairvoyance, clairaudience, and of writing through spirit contact, which is really the higher form of wireless, as it is known to your own world.

Spirit Writing.

When we wish you to learn how to make your vibrations attune themselves to our own it is very necessary that your mind should be free of all extraneous worry, turmoil, and unhealthy, sad, or wicked thoughts. Your ideas must be peaceful, full of understanding of the need for such communications as we are so anxious to send into the world. Then when we are assured of all these points, we are able to set up a very strong current of a kind of electricity between yourself and us, and then the work can be started in real earnest.

It is also very necessary that your body should be quite at ease in its position, as any restriction or want of comfort will cause a kind of mental irritation which acts as a barrier.

Now when all is in order, we send a thought down this wave of so-called electricity and it operates at your end by making words in the language which is most familiar to your ear. Your eye is used to certain characters and your ear to certain sounds, but neither sight nor sound is used by us here, all is made of mental vibrations and your mind receives their equivalent in mind pictures which your world calls words.

(I thought at this point—" We think the word ' cat ' and then picture it—you spirits think the picture ' cat ' and the word follows to us.")

Yes, your idea is very good indeed. Now try for a moment to understand how this works out in other ways. If we think about a subject and tell your hand to write certain words, your hand will write them down, but sometimes your mind is blurred by anger, or fear, or mistrust, or over-anxiety to write correctly, and then this wave gently bends the wrong way and your mind gets wrong words which make no sense at all, or which may even be the entanglement of another person's wave-length after all.

TIME.

When we make errors in names or in time that is because your ideas of time are set in a curious fashion, not easily recognized by us over here. We have no time as you know it. Time is something entirely different, and so we can only say some measure of a period from the angle at which we visualize it over here, and it is very often incorrect.

NAMES.

With regard to names, they are very difficult. Names with us are given for very definite reasons. They are the product of certain degrees of development, or given as a reward in cases of higher consciousness ; but with your own world, they are very often quite haphazard, with no reason at all, and they really do not fit those whom you call by them at all. We give names easily when they exist still in your present state of consciousness, but as a rule not easily if they are entirely new to your own brain.

Q. Do we keep the same name throughout our many incarnations ? I mean in the invisible planes, of course.

A. No, your names are changing with your development over here, and if your work is well done on earth, your name here is one which expresses that work on earth, so you can see that names are very important over here.

In your own world sometimes your ideas about names are quite right, you choose the correct vibrations, but as a rule your choice is entirely at fault and not at all helpful to the one who bears it.

Q. How can you tell whether I have taken this down correctly ?

A. Go on writing a moment longer as we want to prove your writing is correct by our own special methods of testing by your aura. [I continued taking down as they guided my hand.]

You see, certain ideas make certain vibrations and colours round your head, if your mind has correctly written what we have dictated to your mind (and it is this which happens to your hand when your mind contacts ours), then the colours and vibrations give us the ideas back again and we know that your mind has heard correctly.

Now let us tell you about the method we use for making your vibrations tune-in with ours.

When a medium is ready to undertake special work for us we are at once able to set the line of etheric contact vibrating at a very high rate. This is, of course, very like your wireless. If your set is a powerful one, you can get into touch with all kinds of other stations ; but if it is only a very simple one, your own contact will be very limited, as it is in the case of a person who is not very highly tuned-in to spiritual forces. Having set the line in motion we next send our message through, and it will depend on the kind of medium's mind what kind of message we shall send.

CLAIRVOYANCE.

Now, clairvoyance is a gift which can be cultivated, from ordinary simple clairvoyance, such as seeing colour in the atmosphere around you or in people's auras or in your own quiet moments, up to a wonderfully high level of seeing these great visions to which we have already referred. It needs quiet perseverance, prayer, meditation, and always the desire to make progress for the sake of progress and not for material gain. Much is denied those who seek material gain or notoriety, for it is the prostitution of spiritual gifts for unworthy purposes, and as such never attains the real heights which belong only to such as seek wisdom and understanding as that which is above price or earthly advantage.

CLAIRAUDIENCE.

Clairaudience is something of the same, the medium may hear the voices of babblers on the other side, of no special import, or they may hear the voices of angels ; it depends on the tuning-in of their own instruments ; for the educated ear of a musician hears beauties in a passage of music entirely missed by the ignorant. The highly trained clairaudient medium may even consciously attend the councils of Great Beings on these inner planes and take back firsthand teaching as it is given out in his hearing ; that is, of course, extremely rare, but it has been done and will be done again, for in the future, inspirational speaking will be greatly developed in the new age of church teaching.

These three forms of mediumship deal with the higher faculties, even though they may only be developed in the easiest form for the medium's present life on earth, but they all deal with the uses of the higher forces which work through the pineal and pituitary glands.

DIRECT VOICE.

The Direct Voice is, of course, most useful and most convincing, but there again be very careful of this, as many desire to speak who would not speak wisely or truthfully, because they might be earthbound and very ignorant of our true life over here.

If your mind wishes to develop this, your mind must try to understand something of your own system of wireless, as we use this system on a higher level with human throats as the stations for giving off the proper touch of vibration.

You generate a kind of ectoplasm, but it is not really the ordinary kind of materializing ectoplasm, but something subtler ; your throats have to be remodelled in a peculiar manner, which gives your voice an additional sounding-box, as it were, a double throat, as your brain describes it.

MATERIALIZATION.

Now, the mediumship which deals with the magnetic body is a mediumship requiring strict control and very careful discipline of the emotions and desires. It must be perfectly clear to your minds that emanations from this magnetic body may be pure or impure, and a strongly magnetic body may not always mean a good or moral body, so that if a person is evilly inclined then the materializations will not be of a high order, and may even be of a very distinctly evil nature, giving use to the embodiment of astral entities evil, horrible and dangerous. As a rule the higher spiritual entities do not allow themselves to be enmeshed into vehicles of psychic matter thrown off by mediums at the ordinary séance, so that materializations, though very useful for the ordinary practical convincing of the materialist or sceptic, are not regarded over here with any special interest since they lead nowhither at all.

SPIRIT-PHOTOGRAPHY.

The medium for spirit photography is of a better type as a rule, because the emanation sent out is far finer and subtler, and the spirit which impresses itself on the sensitive plate is usually of a better type of advancement over here. It is very useful to us, and is a very extraordinary thing. It will become a very important branch in the near future, as it is very convincing. It is not really a thing that you can set out to develop. Your make-up possesses some quality or it does not ; it is quite a different line of development. Sometimes Guides are very glad to have the opportunity of impressing their appearance in the aura of those whose auras are attached to their own vibrations. Sometimes evidence of a special kind is sent through where there is urgent need for it, but always beware of using this gift, which is a very rare one, lightly or unworthily, or for financial advantage, or it will fail the medium in the end.

The lower forms of mediumship which are attracted by the etheric body are very elemental in expression, such phenomena as rapping, throwing, snatching, table-moving, apports, and so forth ; they are the outcome of development more from the occult point of view because they bring a very elementary spirit entity into touch with the medium. It cannot be helped very often, but where this mediumship becomes a nuisance help should be demanded by the individual by prayer, and if necessary by exorcism, for this mediumship is no good at all and must be discouraged at all cost.

There are other forms of mediumship employed by the occultist of the black orders which are of the etheric and magnetic kinds because they use vile and bestial practices which make certain demands on the genitals and excretory organs, also infusions of blood are used ; these are an abomination before God, and will lead to final destruction of all such dabblers.

[I asked here how a person could find out what was their special psychic faculty ?]

We are very anxious to finish this instruction on mediumship, so please continue writing, and we will make an answer on your question later.

These occult practices are in force even in the present time. We are all perfectly aware of these secret brotherhoods, these travesties of so-called inner wisdom, and we wish to make this definite statement clear to all such as read these pages that there will be a terrible destruction of all perverts, of all workers of black magic, of all those who cause the innocent to commit follies which will lead later on to their defilement.

God is not mocked nor desecrated.

He has an Eye that never closes, and He will surely destroy all those who work filth or any kind of unnatural abominations.

. Hence, ye unclean, forget not your God, but repent and wipe away your abominations from the face of His fair earth.

.   .   .   .   .   .

We will now answer your question. If a man desires to learn how to come into touch with his own particular type of psychic faculty let him first try to find out how his mind turns best towards the higher attainment of perfection, for only real seekers should be aided in this. We do not wish to help those who desire mediumship for personal benefit or notoriety. The faculty will show itself quite unmistakably before he has trained himself in prayer and meditation very long, but of course in a school of preparation which we wish yourselves to start, it will be shown to certain who are already developed, and that will help the enquirer.

K

CHAPTER XVIII

THE WAY OF ATTAINMENT (contd.)

(c) Further Instruction. Type of Medium required. Diet. Contact at
Séances. Trance Mediums.

TYPE OF MEDIUM REQUIRED.

When we find some whose vibrations are easily recognized as being in accord with all our requirements, we set to work to train them by advice, in order to make them fit in every way to receive our messages, which we send through various mediums on our own planes. We do not as a general rule get into direct contact with our physical mediums, as they are not sufficiently advanced at first.

When their minds make the proper contact, we can get into much closer contact and then the work goes very quickly indeed. We do not always know in what way our mediums are going to react to certain stimuli.

The body is first purified of all physical imperfections, such as the physical inclination to make Uric Acid, as that is very bad for us to work through. We must have most pure vessels for pouring our healing through. We need very much healthier mediums. More attempt to make contact should be made with us by prayers, they will always be heard.

When we wish to communicate with your worlds and we want to be sure of making ourselves very clearly understood in what we wish to tell, we choose someone whose vibrations can most easily be made to tune-in with ours, as we do not wish to waste power or time.

It is not very easily done as we make a very high demand on our mediums.

We desire Obedience, more devoted labour than most are prepared to render, and more good works in the general way of life, for Service is one of the finest methods of coming into higher contact with other planes.

Then we also require men and women whose mental equipment is of sufficiently advanced order, so that we may impress what we wish to teach on their brains without any undue tax.

We welcome those who are anxious to avoid publicity of every kind, as we know they will not make mistakes so easily when once trained. To begin with, they are most conscientious, and have no need to work when not in the mood for work. That is all to the good, as they cannot be influenced by other people's emanations in the same way.

You can see that if mediums are not equal to their work at the moment, they may defraud, or, what is more often the case, they may lay themselves open to receive wandering spirits. That is often why mediums are so foolish in what they say. Their own control does not necessarily control all the time, and the intruder may talk nonsense. We much prefer to train our mediums ourselves. If mediums are strong enough to persevere alone, we can always help them on their way by suggestion, advice, diet, and such-like.

DIET.

Diet is a very interesting subject and very important from all points of view, as much may depend on the method of dieting as to the influence which is sent to each individual from the spirit planes.

Know then, that the eating of all flesh food is to be avoided by those whose lives are to be dedicated to the highest form of spiritual life ; but of course discretion must be used in making all drastic changes or ill-health may ensue. Fruit of all kinds is natural and most wholesome, especially fruit of a juicy nature ; not much dried fruit, but nuts, oranges, grapes, apples, sometimes bananas. Much is given in the way of tonic food by the juice of grape-fruit and of oranges ; lemons are very wholesome and limes. Much must depend on the blood condition of the individual as, of course, some may not be able to enjoy the very acid properties of these latter fruits.

Milk foods are very good for over-tired, nervous folk, also eggs. Honey is a queen of foods, which is the reason it was

used by ascetics and all who lived free, wild lives, who were
natural healers, prophets, and such-like. Cooked green food
is not nearly so good as uncooked green stuff; all root
vegetables are good if eaten raw and grated. Cheese is
most nourishing, your brown bread is not so very wholesome
after all, cereals with milk, honey, or fruit are very much
better. Fish gives certain qualities of phosphorus in the
system and is less dangerous than red flesh. Birds are
living, sentient beings, and should not be eaten by such as
lead the higher life; but be very careful not to be too
desperately anxious to alter all your old methods; change
must be very gradual. We know, of course, that when a
new life is entered upon its followers are most anxious
to do what is required by these changes, and we advise
abstention from flesh diet, but wait a time, for all these
changes use common sense.

Q. How do controls of mediums contact our relations
and friends on the other side and get their messages to us?
A. Your friends over here are not actually seen as your
eyes understand this term, but we sense them and we know
when they wish to contact your own spirits through your
earth consciousness. We are always in touch whenever
your souls call to us for assistance, or even when your
thoughts are set on us as your unseen friends, for our
Master is our mutual Friend, and we all work together in
a comradeship, your souls and our spirits, an ever-living
company in much more intimate sense than your minds
suspect.
There is really no such division as death suggests to your
minds; we see, as your minds call it, no special difference
in vibration, and when we convey a message to anyone on
earth from the next plane it is only because there is a very
urgent call for it from your earth or from the next plane.
We sometimes wonder why they bother us, there is so little
between them, after all. When we want to come in touch
ourselves it is because we wish specialized information to
be given, and we only choose those who will best suit our
purposes.
Q. This does not explain what we wish to know.
A. You are making a very common mistake. The
ordinary medium is not under the control of a very high

spirit at all, for such spirits do not utilize their powers on trifling matters. At a séance a medium means that there is a kind of shadow of the loved one present, an emanation from the aura of the questioner, not actually the living spirit-form at all, but a kind of ghost or shade sent to give the medium a sense of their presence in or about those who seek this knowledge of a loved one. It is like a photograph or, let us say in your modern term, a televisual representation, not the friend but a plate or set of vibrations.

Q. Do mediums in trance know what they are saying ?

A. Not always, but much more often than is admitted. It is very difficult to be very accurate on this point, for we really cannot tell whether they are in deep trance or not ; there again we must rely on lower kinds of mediums. We give the necessary vibrations to give certain information, but we have no special interest as to how information gets to your earth, or the exact rate of vibration at which it is carried, so long as it arrives there. When we want information to be received in such a method we usually instruct certain of our mediumistic helpers to give the necessary information, but we are not specially interested in the ordinary methods of conversations between various sets of enquirers such as usually attend the séance room.

CHAPTER XIX

HEALING

THERE is a very great service to be rendered to humanity by the beautiful act and art of healing. The science of it is known to many on your earth plane, but there is a part of which your own medical opinion is very ignorant, and yet, did they but know it, they are often unconscious agents acting under our own healing Guides over here.

Disease and suffering are two of the most common burdens of humanity, and if only more light would be received on the reasons for those burdens and the very simple methods in which very often relief might be obtained, more than half this suffering would and could be avoided. No human being can be at his best, his highest, or his most useful degree of service, if his own bodily sufferings render him conscious of a disharmony between himself and his surroundings. The old Greeks were always right when they insisted on perfect bodily health as the prelude to a higher spiritual life, and no man was ever considered fit for any higher life unless he was of sound body as well as of upright and pure character.

Disease is indeed the great disharmony of Nature ; it is wrong ; it is against the laws of God whence issued all that was rhythmic and harmonious, and it is Man's constant duty to help suffering humanity to re-attune itself to these perfect rhythms by combating disease of all kinds. This cannot be understood unless the real nature of disease is understood, also the reason for individual suffering of illness or deformity, and also something of the laws of reincarnation to which man owes something of the sufferings endured in his present life.

It should be clearly understood that in these inner planes there are several bodies of Healers who, knowing the importance of a healthy humanity, are ever in touch with all who suffer and with all who seek to cure suffering, in order to try to help both in their endeavours to find health.

Many people in your own midst possess the power of healing naturally, either by rays which emanate from their own health aura and from their own magnetic bodies, or by the power of touch, or by the gift of clairvoyance, or by an occult knowledge of herbs and Nature's healing balms. We are in touch with all such, often quite unknown to them ; but many, too, work well and consciously with our various groups, and as your years progress more and more healing will be done through these agents rather than through those doctors who remain hidebound in their old beliefs. We must not decry the work of doctors, many of whom lead most unselfish lives and who struggle bravely against great odds to relieve the stress of human suffering ; but still, there are very many who are obstinate and very cruel in their ways of finding out knowledge, all of which matter will one day be proved to be foolishness, for no lasting good is ever done by methods of cruelty, which is always abhorrent to the Great Father of all sentient life.

In the chapter which we have given on the constitution of the human body it will be noticed that man is composed not only of the heavy dense physical material which your brains designate as flesh, and which your minds foolishly designate as the heir to all suffering and disease, for indeed all suffering emanates from far subtler causes and is merely reflected in the dense physical either during this one life, or part of it, or through a series of other lives. When this new idea is thoroughly understood then will a more reasonable and sensible method of healing be introduced into your earth plane and disease will release its stranglehold on your poor sufferers.

Now, when a man is smitten with illness it would be wise to consider him from the aspect of his own outlook on life ; if it is very depressed, or very malicious, or very selfish, the illness might be typical of that outlook ; it usually is. An ordinary doctor will prescribe for the outward physical ill, but who shall minister to a mind or soul diseased ?

Q. In the case of epidemics, say influenza, or of measles, whooping-cough, and so forth, which children get, even young babies, how can these minds be ministered to ?

A. This is a very sensible question, because this subject of children's illness appears most incomprehensible. Truly a babe is an innocent sufferer, and these illnesses you mention are so-called childish complaints, but has it not yet occurred to your mind that your children are not born into your world for the first time, and that each brings with it a body already pledged to suffer certain ills which circumstance will render serious or innocuous as the child's case merits, or as the Mother shall deserve ?

Epidemics are caused by mental or moral illness in the inner planes. Men's souls are sick, their mentality stunted, ill-grown, cramped, evil, and from these mental planes a kind of miasma is set up which interpenetrates your earth planet as an epidemic of a sickness of the physical body ; but a beautiful soul, a clean mentality, will not suffer as a rule unless there is a reason for cutting short the life by some ordinary method of human destruction. But the ordinary wholesome-minded person has a clean bill of health and a very healthy effect on all who come within his aura. Those who sap the vitality of others with whom they live in daily contact protect their [own] physical lives, it is true, but they will suffer one day in another life for this form of selfishness. So do not forget that not only must a man be healthy himself, but he must emanate health too, otherwise he is in reality a sick person.

Now, we have said that when we choose out persons to train them as mediums we sometimes have to cleanse their system of latent impurity ; such is the case with all who have lived lives in crowded cities, or who have lived on wrong diet, or who have inherited certain physical weaknesses ; these we render sick in order to cure them and in order to stimulate their vitality and purify their auras ; but they are quite different from the ordinary sick or diseased persons ; it is for these latter people that we wish this subject of healing to be better understood.

.   .   .   .   .   .

METHODS OF HEALING.

The Pearl Ray.

We made your mind aware of what we must call the Pearl Ray. It is a soft, silvery colour, rather like moonlight, or moonstones, pearls, or whatever best conveys to your mind the sense of a soft iridescence. Some already possess it and use it ; some have it but do not know it ; others have no idea of its existence at all. It emanates from the possessor unconsciously, and at will may be directed much as a torchlight may be switched on to a person by focussing the will-power on the patient for whom this ray is to be released.

The possessors cannot use it on their own persons—it goes forth from them—virtue goes out of them, as it were, and when in good health there it is, always available ; but it flags during extreme fatigue, or may be overstrained by too much diffusion. It is a very subtle ray, and is carried through subtler matter than ether.

Q. Is ether solid or extremely subtle ?

A. It is solid in the sense that it sustains the universe. Your earth rests in it. It is subtle, in that it interpenetrates all sentient life, and is necessary to all that has form.

This pearl ray is a kind of atmosphere or magnetic emanation, subtler than your etheric body or health aura ; but it functions through it ; is an extra layer of matter surrounding the magnetic body, when at its best. It is destructive and yet life-giving ; it destroys evil, and builds up or reconstitutes good tissue in the physical body, and invigorates and stimulates the demagnetised mental body. It is a very useful gift, it should be strengthened by harmonious living and cleanliness in life on all planes of existence.

Q. Can a person who possesses it destroy it ? Or a person who desires it, acquire it ?

A. Impurity of life will naturally destroy it in time, but it is not easily acquired ; it seems to be possessed by some who take it back to their earth lives, because they possessed certain powers of healing in a former incarnation. We know of no case of a fresh acquisition of this ray in the present lives of any who possess it at the moment.

As we have said, the ray is a kind of ectoplasm, for which there is so far no special name in the scientific world, but one day they will discover it, and then they will make all the use they possibly can of those who already possess it.

Q. Will they be able to manufacture it or will they have to depend on those who have it already ?

A. They will make the discovery in a very curious way. They will find that there is an emanation from certain people, which can heal at a distance, and that will make them very curious to use it on special cases. This ray may be used in all cases of diseased tissue. Those possessing it should make a mental picture of the afflicted part, and direct the ray as though it were a kind of lamp with a special light on to the diseased part.

Q. Can this be done in the presence of the patient as well as in his absence ? How long must one concentrate ?

A. In the case of absent treatment the ray may be given to us at night, with your demand that we shall use it for a certain patient ; or, if preferred, as in very urgent cases of bad illness, make a circle of light round the patient and then use the ray for a few moments' most earnest concentration.

For treating patients when in your own aura it is necessary to place your hands on the afflicted part, or, at any rate, hold their hands for the space of another few moments, this sets up a very strong current.

Healing by Magnetic Passes ; by absent Mental Treatment.

This method is very good for nervous troubles and for cases when ray treatment is not required, as it is not suitable for all kinds of ailments. In some cases ray treatment would be a very great waste of good force. You can learn to discriminate quite easily.

For Mental Healing.

If you wish to make a strong magnetic current for mental healing, your brain must concentrate on mental healing on every occasion. Make mental pictures of the person you wish to heal and send a current of magnetic thought, full of sympathy and understanding (however wrong that person may be in his life), and this current will act as a deterrent ; he will not react at once, but use prayer and patience, it will win in the end. Magnetic passes must always be properly taught by a competent healer who works along these lines.

Mixed Treatment.

Sometimes a mixture of two is desirable, this is usually when the nervous illness is the result of wrong ideas or fears, or some kinds of diseases, which are the outcome of too much thought about self, and both are very similar in the result on the human body.

Healing by Prayer.

When your minds pray to heal, your aura at once sets waves of power in motion. Rays, too beautiful to express in your own dull language, are set in long currents like coloured streamers of light which go out towards the sufferers and enwrap them in bands of healing radiance. Yes, indeed, prayer is very powerful in all ways.

Your aura is really the extent of your sympathy ; that is the reason why healers have very extended auras : their desire to relieve suffering brings out a very wonderful radiation which can vibrate indefinitely through space.

Now, when your prayers draw our attention to a case, we set up a line of communication between your patient, yourself, and ourselves. This creates a very powerful current of healing power, and we are then made to conclude our work by sending your force through. Much is done over here in the way of thought, as we then know what kind of healer to put into touch with the case.

HEALING BY CLAIRVOYANT DIAGNOSIS.

We wish to tell your readers something about the method of healing by clairvoyant diagnosis.

This is a very useful method, as naturally there is no chance of making grievous mistakes, or giving false diagnoses.

Now when a healer has become clairvoyant, he will notice that around each physical body there is a kind of luminous sheath of tiny projecting rays, which give the body the appearance of a hedgehog ; and again beyond this, beyond and interpenetrating, there is a kind of cloud of coloured matter—the aura— which tells us much about the character.

Now do not confuse the aura with the astral body, they influence one another truly ; the astral body is an actual body which separates itself from the main physical body and gives a life apart from the outer man, in sleep, in death state, or under the influence of drugs, drink, or anæsthetics. The aura gives the colour to the astral, much in the same way that racial influences and blood give the colouring to the physical body.

Now the clairvoyant sees both these emanations if he is properly advanced, though some only see the etheric or health aura ; this merely shows the seat of the injury, the aura will show the cause.

Now let us suppose the health aura shows the unhealthy discoloration of a lung, the colour of the aura will be very dirty too in that region. The actual density will show whether this injury belongs to the present life, or to a past one, and the general colouring of the whole aura will give the direction to be followed.

Here obviously the healer must use his hands for magnetic healing and whenever possible the pearl ray, a most cleansing and revivifying ray, only, alas ! so rare in your world. Disease needs a killing out of poisoned tissue and the aura needs stimulating by prayer, fresh air, sunshine, suitable food.

Always remember that stimulation of the aura and of the health sheath is most efficacious in all cases ; it is like shaking up a bottle with a sediment. Everybody becomes stagnant after a time, shake them up and teach them to shake themselves up too. A few sensible physical exercises —a few deep breaths of fresh air—a few glasses of cold water—a few words of spiritual inspiration—how extremely simple, and yet how magnificently efficacious !

The clairvoyant healer must always study the patient's character, mental inertia, or mental activity on the wrong lines ; dear, dear, there you have the seeds of poisoned blood, the root of rheumatism, neuritis and many of the ills which man glibly describes as his heritage.

Man was meant to be healthy and happy, and the sooner

he begins to believe it, the better for himself, his children, and the world in general.

Now, when we are considering a case over here, we naturally can see the whole character and past lives of the patient, and we know that there are certain kharmic laws with which we may not interfere ; here we may only give amelioration and this helps considerably. If a patient has brought on sickness by his own evil habits or by malicious thoughts, then, as a rule, we do not help. But if it is the case of accident, or of some unhappy circumstances in which the patient is a victim, or caught in the web of his own fate, but where he is really trying to be a good fellow, then we can always help, and we do, sometimes by suggesting to his doctor a change of treatment, sometimes by suggesting a change of doctor to the patient.

In cases where we are directly asked to help and where we have suitable physical mediums, we are enabled to work on our own lines. It is a fact that future generations will benefit more and more by these methods of healing. This art has always existed in all schools of religion and existed no less in the Christian.

Jesus was one of the best healers your world has ever known, and He advocated healing, but with singular obstinacy your Church has crushed all such endeavours from its midst.

Never mind, it will return before many years have passed over your heads.

It is above all things necessary that the healer should be a very clean living and a very healthy person, not an eater of flesh foods or a drinker of intoxicating beverages, which always lay the regular eater or drinker open to attack from undesirable entities and weaken the morale of the healer.

Participation in drugs, alcoholic beverages, red-blooded flesh foods, is at the root of an enormous amount of disease in your present day. Alcohol should be regarded as a medicine, for it is a very good one, but nothing else.

These remarks are only stray hints on a very big subject. We need healing mediums badly ; but, dear people, we need intelligent ones above all ! Healing is a science just as much as medicine or surgery, and the healer is a born humanitarian with a big fund of sympathy, a fund of humour, and a practical knowledge of the ordinary physical body and a practical knowledge of herbs and simple natural remedies.

HEALING BY KNOWLEDGE OF THE PAST.

You must begin to understand now at last the very wonderful connection there is between a man's body and the powers of the Great Oversoul, and in time your mind will grasp what is really behind disease.

All parts of your body are linked up with great natural forces, the great creative and elemental forces in Nature, that when your brain has grasped these points more fully, your mind will follow the natural sequence of ideas that if a man's soul or spirit is deficient in certain qualities, he will show signs of that defection by a corresponding physical weakness, or he will be attacked by a sudden illness which has some connection with this.

Take for example your own early sufferings from headache.[1] They were mostly due to a suppression of your natural mental output of energy. It poisoned your blood, making it poor and thin. Your own doctors called it rheumatism and anæmia, and so it was, but the cause was spiritual in its essence. Your past lives were full of a certain kind of debt. Your soul had betrayed what was strictly forbidden and in your present life the time had come for your soul to finish paying off that overdraft. Your soul was really long in advance of your outward physical life. Your mind sighed in captivity, it languished in a hated prison, and all this collected and streamed into your physical body and your head received no real relief until your psychic development was allowed to start.

A weak digestion is often the outward sign of errors in the judgment of a soul in its past lives. The wrong has generally been in the wrongful treatment of those whom the soul has loved.

Anyone who suffers from cancer or any kind of malignant growth, your mind may rest assured that in some past life there has been an unlawful use of the human functions, such as sex abuse or sexual faults of some kind. Yes, cancer denotes abuse of sex functions, not in a very recent life, perhaps, and certainly not in the case of a person of very

---

[1] I wished to omit this, but was bidden to leave it as it stood—M.B.

moral character in his present life : it is a long outstanding debt and will be wiped out entirely and for ever.

Your mind must not be horrified at this remark when your mind remembers those of your friends whose bodies have been destroyed by this type of illness in this life ; for remember, all life is but a payment of past mistakes, or a reward for past accomplishment of good deeds. It is necessary to be fully aware of these little-known details, if you are to understand the deeper issues involved in healing. Healing work will not be so much on the surface as it appears if more were known of the fundamental reason for illness and disease of all kinds.

In diagnosis it is necessary to understand what is wrong with the individual mind first. For instance, when you meet a child suffering from disease of any organ of the body, such as eyes, nose, or of the blood or skin, or having distorted joints or crippled limbs, your mind must dwell on the past indicated by these symptoms. The child, we will say, has bad limbs. Well then in a former life it was a very immoral man or woman, and in this case you see the sins being worked out in the third or fourth incarnation, not " generation " as your own scriptures have written it.

Q. Why then bother to cure cases which rouse one's pity ?

A. That is a very wise question and we will try to answer it clearly.

When a child is born deformed or has any terrible defect, although it has brought it over with other debts from its own past, it has also brought with it certain rights, also earned in its past ; probably rights obtained through the higher part of its nature even in those remote days. These rights may be paid off on the credit side by a linking-up with certain influences which may heal ; or it may only be able to link up with some influence which will ameliorate the conditions ; or it may have to endure the curse all its life.

Healing power is given to certain mediums, whether spiritualists or orthodox doctors, and they being gifted in this manner ought to use these gifts whenever events lead them into contact with those who suffer. The very fact that a child is given a chance to be cured is a sign that they have already been placed in the way of the necessary help.

All healers are workers with Christ the great Healer, even if they apparently do not recognize His divine powers, and when you are shown where help is needed then be sure the person or child requiring the help is by right of some merit in the past due to be helped.

Q. If they are healed promptly how do they manage to pay off the debt which they bring over with them ?

A. They bring the debt it is very true, but they also bring a credit, and if they can pay off the debt early in life so much the better for them.

Q. I cannot understand why it should be necessary to know this back-history of the child. If I met a sick or diseased child I should naturally desire to cure it ; I should not be a bit interested in its past errors and my knowing them surely would not help the child ?

A. That is also a wise question. But although your mind may be set on curing the body, your mind must also try to stir the subtler vibrations of the past, which are always attached to the past. Healing is not altogether external only, it is a very fine internal or hidden science, and if your mind realizes this, it will not be so content with merely healing the body ; it will attempt to stir the latent qualities of the soul to greater vigilance or care.

Neurasthenia, epilepsy, insanity, mania, and such-like cases are, of course, very interesting from a mental plane point of view, and we must admit that your doctors understand them very little indeed. How should they ? They are seldom spiritualists and if they were they would have to conceal the fact.

All kinds of mental cases are usually due to the wrongful use of drugs, drink, and also of occult practices on bad or evil lines in a former life. They bring back to the earth a very feeble etheric body and all kinds of evil mentalities from the spirit world batten on these poor creatures. Only the understanding of disentanglement of their cramped bodies can effect the proper change, and much can be done by those who understand addressing themselves to the possessing entity, commanding it to depart ; exorcism is a true thing to understand. The healer must guard himself against the released spirit when endeavouring to rid a body of evil obsession or possession.

Now, of course, those illnesses such as consumption, ills

of the respiratory organs, are very easily dealt with if taken in time, as they do not indicate very deadly sins in the past at all. They indicate more obvious faults of temperament. These illnesses are usually sent as trials of patience and courage ; bad cases are curiously cheerful and patient, they have learnt their lesson well.

Nervous diseases such as neuritis, sciatica, are purely mental diseases if only your doctors realized this fact. The patient has not accumulated sufficient self-control, or sometimes a sudden increase of mental tension sets up bad muscular conditions. Lack of mental interest in life is a very frequent cause of this class of illness.

In fact character and disease are most closely connected, so that given a man's character you may know also what kind of illness he is likely to suffer from.

HEALING CIRCLES.

Healing is very much a matter of concentration of prayers and mind control for which groups are most suited, as they combine forces and direct them where needed. Much can be done by these means but there are other methods which require special gifts, such as rays, magnetic currents ; also powers of diagnosing either by touch or by sighting clairvoyantly how the aura shows itself. This is particularly interesting as you can help the patient in other difficulties. Much disease is caused by sinful thinking, some by mistakes made in past lives, some by sheer ignorance of thought. Many healers do not know enough about these matters so do not make the best of their gifts. You will learn to discriminate with practice ; try to cultivate a very keen sense of touch, it will help vastly. A healing circle should put itself into touch with as many sick people as possible and notice how the vibrations vary with each one.

Q. When concentrating on absent treatment is it best to nominate the patient or visualize him if known ?

A. Your friend's question is very sensible indeed. Your best method is to find out the name of the patient, this establishes a link in the ether of space and we make contact between the patient whom your mind desires to help, then we can diagnose his ailment and put him in charge of the healer most suitable over here, or with some one specially

L

interested in him. But if the name is not known your mind has no very direct means, this may mean that the many currents are deflected away from the patient, and the best method to be employed is a general prayer for those whose interest this patient has become. Your prayers are never wasted, they always affect some one in the aura of the enquirer.

Q. Is prayer sufficient or should one concentrate on the ailment or on his health ?

A. Your minds have the power to remove ailments, your prayers can always put the patient in touch with our healers. Make a strong mental effort willing the ailment to break down, the health will generally follow or the pain be relieved.

CHAPTER XX

COLOUR

Planetary Influences. Orange. Yellow. Red. Green. Blue. Amethyst.
What underlies Colour ? Law of Signatures.

KNOW then, that this subject of colour is of vast importance
and if rightly understood amongst your own people there
would be an immense benefit able to be used at any moment
by all such as could apply this colour science to everyday
life. It is, of course, very well understood that certain
colours rouse certain vibrations in the human aura, because
naturally the human emanations are very sensitive and
most easily influenced by the vibrations which match, as
it were, the rate of vibration already existing in their own
aura. Thus if a man be fiery and much given to headstrong
argument his colour would probably be something which
corresponds to the vibration of red ; therefore red would
very easily excite him more. But a man used to more
peaceful and useful ways would probably emanate green in
some shade or other, and green would be a colour which
would very easily tone in with his particular vibrations.

In the case of blue the psychic faculty is more or less
awakened and a man would do well to encourage the love
of this colour if his everyday life were not too actively
strenuous, for it is a colour which acts as a sedative.

Orange or yellow colours are very stimulating ; the man
who needs his material life to improve should have yellow
about him, but orange if he chooses public speaking or
lecturing, as it is an occult colour and helps to protect the
wearer from the evils which might assail him in public work.

A rich purple or amethyst is the best colour for those
who lead the people's spiritual life.

Now, of course, it is not easy to tell men and women that
they should wear or use certain colours for certain results,

163

because the everyday life of people would hardly permit these peculiarities; your people do not live where the study of colours is part of the everyday life. Your blacks and greys and browns and dark dismal shades are wretched and very depressing indeed; but it would be perfectly possible to encourage colour in the everyday surroundings, in the home, in the garden, and where possible in the clothing.

But it will be very much more possible in the future to treat illnesses with coloured rays of light, that has already been discovered, and as time goes on it will be the best cure for all nervous complaints and for many diseases in the blood which at present baffle your medical men. Rays, rather than drugs, that will be the medicine of the future; organisms of evil nature will be split up and dissolved by rays of suitable strength and colour.

Now this subject of colour is not very well advanced in your world because it is very little realized how many colours exist in your very midst which are not seen by the ordinary eye, for if once the gift of clairvoyance became a very much more developed faculty than it is now, then each could see for himself the effects of colours on auras, and the subtle changes in an aura when stirred by contact with other auras, or when fined by the refining influences of prayer, meditation, and spiritual striving.

The general appearance in a public building of auras is very dull, very indifferent, and very few stand out in the thick gloom, but when they do they effect changes all round them. In cases where a dispute is in course of being talked out, there are often very ugly effects of forked lightning in ugly reds, browns, greens, blacks; but when during a religious service, or when a person delivers a spiritual address, the auric mass in the building becomes much more transparent, soft colours suffuse the individuals and much temporary good is done by such an influence.

Now when persons become aware of colour they should endeavour by quiet concentration to make this faculty grow, it will undoubtedly; let them concentrate on their own aura, then on the auras of those nearest them, and by degrees they will find that the power grows and they will enter another dimension of space and find that every man, woman, and child, has a very distinct colour emanation, and much will be learned of their characters and personal

needs ; above all, much will be revealed about each person's
health.

The health aura must not be confused with the higher
spiritual aura, but a very healthy and mentally well-balanced
person, as a rule, has the elements of a better, clearer, and
clearly defined spiritual aura. Now this question of the
health aura properly belongs to our chapter on healing, so
for the present we will pursue the idea of colour in its more
general effect and this is already in your existing instructions.

Colour is a very occult subject, although it is very little
realized as such ; it makes the mind respond to certain
vibrations in the scheme of creation and it has a very
singular effect on the human body in particular, for it
stimulates or depresses, brings calm, restful thoughts to the
mind, or makes it very restless and excitable. Each person
will react to the vibrations of colour quite differently from
his neighbour, and one person cannot choose the colour for
another person.

Q. Is it not the case that the colour most becoming to a
person is the right colour for him ?

A. Yes to a certain extent this is a general rule, but
there are certain colours which should never be used by
certain people at all. When the planetary influences are
not in harmony with the colours chosen, they should not be
worn, they ill-become the personality and that is just what
your physical eyes cannot tell.

Q. Can you tell us how the correct planetary colours can
be found out ?

A. The planetary influences are decided by the well
drawn-up horoscope, but it is not everyone who calls himself an astrologer who can do this.

It is very simple really ; the planetary influence is best
decided by the vibration of the person's birth number and
his name number, but the birth number is the best, because
names are often given foolishly and incorrectly ; the
correct colour is not the colour of the ruling planet, but the
complementary colour ; for instance, red is the colour of
Mars, or what your eyes know as red (not red as we know it).
Well, never tell a person who is ruled by Mars to wear red,
it is an added stimulant to a very restless and fiery temper.
Suggest green, it will subdue these tendencies.

The real art of horoscope reading is knowing how to give the information as guidance that helps the person to overcome unfortunate tendencies.

The planetary influence of the sun is very very powerful ; the colour is gold and all shades of bright colours in orange, browns and all shades of copper ; they are rich colours giving energy, warmth, and very gratefully comforting to those whose blood does not keep them very warm. It is a most protective colour too.

Yellow, golden colours, orange and light bright copper, bronze, browns, are most healthful colours, invigorating, stimulating, yet not in any really bad ways, as red might very easily become. All such colours have an effect on the mental body, and if a person has these colours very outstanding in their auras, it shows mental qualities rather than spiritual, though it is well to have these colours, as it will give the necessary intellectual grasp of brain quality, most necessary to all writers, speakers, and to all who have to push onward in the world, where speech should always be golden.

Those who react to these colours most easily are those who can express themselves ably and easily, for the reaction of the colour vibration approaches more nearly to the sound vibrations in intensity or rapidity. Yellow is a most interesting vibration, because it links up the occult centres with these greater unseen forces in nature, forces which are power giving, and very potent in rousing the slumbering faculties in the novice.

The orange-coloured robe was purposely chosen by the Eastern occultist to attract these outer forces to his own inner self ; and orange, brilliant and warming, remains the best colour for protecting and stimulating this particular part of men's bodies. It should not be worn by those who fear occult things ; it should always be somewhere in the neighbourhood of those who seek union with these forces. Yellow is very predominant in nature, because in nature the occult forces are very strongly developed.

Take care of your auburn-headed children, they are very susceptible to all occult forces, and are very sensitive, as a rule, unless they have strongly marked counterbalancing signs.

Yellow and orange are part of the same vibration, but yellow is a little more subtle than orange. Orange is very invigorating, but yellow is highly intellectual and is found in the auras of those whose mentality is well advanced but not so forward in contacting outside influences. Yellow gives individual study and intellect, the orange vibration gives the intellect that teaches others.

RED.

Red is the true danger sign of your own earth planet, your own minds have already grasped this, for red is used as a danger signal in all your ideas of human safety and well-being. Try not to let red rule your thoughts if ever your nerves are tired or irritable.

You can understand the curious freak of mind which brings about what is called by your people blood lust ; it is caused by overstimulation of the red colouring matter in their own bodies, which reacts to the red rays unseen yet permeating the ether around your bodies and earth plane. This results in the attraction of like to like, and the unfortunate beings, stimulated by these red rays, demand yet more and more red stimulant, so that they see red, smell red, hear red, and red alone will satisfy this unwholesome demand in their own bodies ; and wars, revolutions, bloody sports, bloody rites, blood food, are demanded by the red vibration at its crudest. Remember that is how red affects your own earth planet, but it is not so with other beings. Red is the finest and noblest kind of vibration in other lines of evolution, hence your ideas of red, the softer tones of red, rose, pink, and such like, being modified into vibrations of the kingly office, the sacrifice of Divine Love at its highest.

GREEN.

Now turn gladly to green and refresh both heart and mind with the reaction toward this colour-vibration—joy in the quiet pulses of awaking spring fills your soul with the strange languors of spring. That is why spring, as your people call it, has the curious effect on the human bodies, it retards the action of vibration, and leads the thoughts in other directions. The red vibrations in each human body are being tempered by the quiet vibrations of the newly awakening vibrations of green.

Spring does not really increase your vibrations, it retards them. Your bodies demand green food, and nature provides it in plenty all about you, yet your people hardly recognize how many green foods are waiting to be used in your fields and hedgerows. Your old herbalists were very much wiser than your modern cooks and doctors.

These are very simple ideas ; one day we will tell you something about the minerals and other interesting points, but that is better understood by the true occultist, and we do not write this book for the occultist.

BLUE.

Now turn to the beautiful colour blue, a most inspiring colour—pure, peaceful, apart from mere earthly vibrations, yet most closely connecting man's body with the vibrations of our own spheres. Happy the man whose aura contains much blue ; his intuition, his inspiration are alive and working harmoniously with his psychic body. The reaction of blue on the human body is, of course, really marvellous, and quite equal to the contact of the best magnetic forces artificially applied. Blue is not the highest devotional colour, that is amethyst, but no one can have attained any degree of spirituality without a really wonderful vibratory response to the all-pervading blue of the ether around and through your bodies and your earth plane.

Remember like attracts like, and it is not necessary, really, to be where your eyes feast on blue waters, blue skies, and blue flowers, though they may be an extra help. The human bodies may react to the all-pervading blue vibrations even in a prison or a living hell on earth, for the awakening soul may generate its own colours by attracting them from out the unseen. They are always there, waiting to be used ; just as your atmosphere is full of sounds waiting to be caught into your wave-lengths, and transmitted to your ears by your wireless set. Think blue. Does that seem strange ? And yet so true it is, that the very fact of having blue in your minds can affect those whom your bodies meet in everyday life. Thinking blue can be accomplished by stimulating your spiritual body by prayer, meditation, and by rousing your slumbering intuition.

AMETHYST.

Amethyst is, of course, a very spiritual colour and very rarely seen in the aura of a mere intellectual mind and heart. It is the colour of something transcendent in beauty of thought and idea.

Reason underlies all those colours which are established for certain uses in the world of men.

Why is the grass green, the sky blue, the blood red, the sun yellow, the moon silver, and so on ? These are questions which might arise in your mind ; for why not red grass, blue earth, green fire, and a violet-coloured moon ? Has it ever seemed strange that these colours should all be properly fixed and more or less unalterable ? The reasons are very interesting, for they open another vista before your minds. Now when your eye is seeing red, it is responding to a certain strength or quickness of vibration, which is communicated to the instrument specially tuned-in to receive it, and this tuning-in will, of course, cause certain reactions in your own minds or in your emotions ; thus red will call for a very quick moving response.

Now with regard to colour, we suggested that red was a very quickly moving colour with reference to vibration, for it is the rate of vibration which really decides colour. Try to imagine what would be the effect if all your colours were rearranged in the kingdom of Nature ; red grass and trees, green sky, blue earth and so forth. The effect would be startling because the rate of vibration would be upset rather than your customary outlook. Red grass and trees would have the effect of intense irritation on the mind, and very few would retain sanity, probably no man would be really sane at all. Yet red is the colour of much that is beautiful in your lives, and a ruling colour, since it is the colour of blood, the colour of regal power. It is the colour which in your aura represents the love qualities, from soft tones to the ugly dull red of jealous love, even hatred, the perversion of the love faculty. Red is the strongest stimulant in colour and should be used guardedly.

170 MAN MADE PERFECT

But green is just the opposite, so restful, so full of confidence, of hope ; the reaction to green is most reliable in all cases of restlessness. Green, the sweet calm peacefulness of green, this ray will send your mind to sleep ; think of green glades, green trees, green grass, your vibrations are quickly lowered. No one who calls green his favourite colour will ever be found to be the initiator of a scheme, these make excellent nurses and serve others really well.

Your mind wonders why the flowers have different colours, the butterflies, the birds, and all those beings in Nature, which appear to lead lives on the same lines one with the other. It is very simply answered, because each flower, butterfly, and bird is really tuned-in to different vibrations, and the variety depends on their rate of vibration to the larger schemes of evolution.

Take for example a blue flower, a blue butterfly, a blue bird, and the colour blue in the spectrum, the colour as it really is, not as your limited eyes see it. Now all these vibrate on an especial string or note of divine harmony, and they are produced by the vibration manipulated by that special Being-in-charge of that special note in the realms of Nature's ministering Devas.

You cannot understand this, and it is not so very easy, because you have lost the understanding of the laws of signatures in Nature, that is the strange yet beautiful law that showed man how to apply these secret arts to his own personal advantage, for his own advancement.

Now this law is everywhere visible to the human eye, but it is blinded by long periods of disuse. When a man tried to help his mind to vibrate to a given sound, or colour, he chose a flower of the colour which was necessary for his own needs, and contemplating it in a kind of ecstasy or state of self-hypnosis, he could tune-in to the desired note and vibration, and get into the desired contact. All flower forms are symbols of ideas from the inner plane whence ideas emanate. If your mind wished to dwell on the universal chalice or cup of divine essence of existence, the flower which showed this symbol in its form and colour would be an apt illustration of that which was to be the subject of your profoundest meditation. Your eyes are caught by your own sweet crocus ; it is a chalice or cup, typical of the upspringing life-essence of the new year of external or physical growth ; it is usually the first, and the colours blue, golden, and white ; you can quickly sense their inner meaning. Remember all families of flowers are built upon numbers, form, and colour, so was the divine teaching in the school of the Master Pythagoras. Number is creative, he taught. Know then that this law of signatures is very useful to understand, and in the past it was clearly understood by those who worked miracles, as your own people wrongly call these occurrences. They were not really marvels at all, they were only events following the use of certain laws, which every real occultist and everyone advanced in spiritual knowledge understood and practised.

When a man was sick of some special complaint the wise man or the healer could effect a cure by making use of certain herbs, which corresponded in vibration with the nature of his complaint. Each herb vibrates to a number, and the number, if used correctly, and tuned-in to the sufferer's vibration, could effect a cure. This is, of course, how the use of so-called spells, love-potions, and so forth came into existence ; these were the remains of a profound occult science, formerly most powerful, but now grossly misunderstood. " For every ill there is a balm in Nature."

Many of the old secret societies practised healing on these lines, and made very wonderful cures, but much was lost to mankind through the improper use of knowledge. The art of secret poisoning was a later development of this knowledge of herbs, and of Nature's hidden powers.

When you think of miracles nowadays, your scientific knowledge assumes entire control, and only what can be outwardly proved in the scientific laboratory is accepted by the world in general. It is scarcely to be wondered at, for it appears all very clearly proved fact, though time often proves these facts wrong or inconclusive.

Many years hence this old science will revive, and mankind will be cured by the understanding of the simple laws of signatures, by rays and by herbs.

If your minds could fathom these mysteries, if they could learn to vibrate consciously with Nature's varied vibrations, yourselves could perform miracles too, it is only a matter of faith and courage.

PART III

THE NEW FAITH

" Till we all come in the unity of the faith, and of the knowledge of the Son of God, unto a perfect man, unto the measure of the stature of the fulness of Christ."

CHAPTER XXI

REINCARNATION

Freedom of Choice. Reason for Rebirth. The Amulet of Lives.

THERE is a very great truth which above all things must be taken back into the consciousness of your present-day minds, and that is the subject known as the theory of Reincarnation. It is, however, not a theory, but a veritable fact, known in all mystery teachings in the past, known to all Guides above a certain grade of advancement, and known to very many in your world at the present time. The subject of Reincarnation is at this present time little understood by people amongst the Western or white races.

All mystery teachings made it known to the followers of the various schools, because every school of inner wisdom possessed this inner knowledge of the soul, and all knowledge which makes a very special study of the soul is naturally perfectly aware of the various experiences which every soul must pass through before any degree of advancement towards perfection is attained. If your own mystery teaching had not been lost out of your own churches, there would be no need to reintroduce this fact broadcast to the world.

" Ye must be born again," said your Master Jesus, and your minds have only seen the birth of the soul again, a kind of revolution in the one life on earth, but such was not the case. When the soul is born afresh in another body, it has again the chance to become purified and perfected, and all mystical experiences (like the birth into a new form of a young child) are full of responsibilities of working swiftly towards the soul's final release from physical rebirth.

You must know then that what we term the main part of the world is a kind of OVERSOUL, and that is the only thing which will remain when the physical things are passed away. When a man is going to die, the whole of his own life and character is placed on a kind of tablet or glyph or cartouche in subtle matter, inscribed with certain symbols which are a record of the life he is just about to leave behind. These tablets are the man's mind pictures when he wishes to go to the earth again as a newly-born child, and are worn by the soul as a kind of amulet ; so the man is in reality wearing his many incarnations like a necklace of many beads—the spirits are able to read these tablets and can tell the man much about his former lives.

Reincarnation is an experience of much interest, for the soul makes its own conditions entirely voluntarily ; it has free will and knows what is necessary for its own development in a physical body, for remember that a physical form is one of the greatest of all tests of a soul's real progress towards a goal.

One soul will choose misery, poverty, and know that it will make progress best on these lines ; for by poverty and misery the mind makes contact with all the lowest expressions of physical matter and human experience. If a soul is really wise it will learn these means of progress earlier in its experience, for it will go on from lowest to highest in a splendid upward gradation ; but of course, souls are not always so wise, and the physical body may stultify the soul's growth for several lives, which is a very grave pity.

That will account for the phenomenon of the sudden rise of great men from very humble origins.

Now, it may be that a soul may desire all the sensual joys of your earth plane ; well, they are soon as dust and ashes, and the soul wearies of unwisely stimulated senses, for the senses should be ruled, not be rulers. The senses are the links between your own world and ours. They may be refined to the extent of becoming so sensitive that the psychic faculties are cultivated to the highest uses, and then man becomes seer, teacher, healer, prophet, saviour, and all is made clear to his wonderfully advanced consciousness. On the other hand, he may use these faculties vilely, and be in danger of hell fire, which is not merely a figure of speech but a real spiritual experience on planes of coarser astral and mental matter.

Let us imagine for a moment that a soul desires fame,

which is an ennobling factor sometimes, for fame may often mean that the man's life is spent in hardships and trials of all kinds in order to attain a perfect ideal.

The culminating point is not necessarily a selfish one, it may be something achieved which will benefit the human race.

That is much better than an idle kind of self-depreciation, for ambition may be perfectly and logically worthy in every way. The results of such worthy ambition will bring their own reward, the soul will expand, the man's influence will be very much enlarged, and he will leave the earth-plane very much better for his temporary stay in it.

On the other hand, unworthy ambition will bring its own devastating conclusions, and the man may sink back for an incarnation or two.

Now, it may be that a man or woman may desire to render service to their country or to the great human family, then he or she will have to be prepared to give up all and follow this self-appointed ideal along its thorny path, for the way of all reformers is set round with unsuspected barriers and obstacles ; but the soul has chosen the highest life of all, and he or she will one day enter into the joy of the Master whom your people call the Christ, for Jesus Christ was the most complete embodiment of a saviour, and a saviour is one who saves for eternity those whose own souls might so easily become enmeshed in the follies and evils of the mortal life on earth.

No one who seriously desires to help is ever rejected, work is always found for workers, but the worker must be conscientious in all ways, and may not take responsibilities to drop them whenever the mood takes him.

That is a lesson which must be strenuously inculcated in any school for training souls along the way of spiritual attainment. Freedom in service, but also service which is carried out as though held by the most rigid laws by which labour is rendered for payment : no desire for reward, no hankering after praise, but the cheerful carrying out of self-imposed tasks for the benefit of those less fortunate than themselves.

Now let us take the soul that desires wisdom and understanding. This is a very worthy kind of desire, for wisdom is the flower of the soul of many incarnations, but, of course,

M

wisdom has a side which may be very selfish, and desire only to attain knowledge for selfish ends.

Never keep back any knowledge which may help a fellow being, never accumulate wisdom just to ponder over in the privacy of your own heart, such wisdom will turn to dust and ashes.

Let all wisdom sweeten your soul and enlighten the souls of those whose lives are even now struggling towards the light in the heavenly mansions.

Beware how your mind contacts wisdom of the unseen forces. Beware how your vibrations react to that which comes to your minds out of the unseen.

It may be useful, pure, and very wonderful knowledge ; it may be tinged with evil forces and all so fascinatingly covered that the soul may not hear the warning bell. But prayer and a very sincere desire for wisdom and not for power will always prevent any serious disaster.

Remember we guard the portal of all entrances into the hidden ways of Nature, and none may pollute her chastity by evil thought, desires, or selfishness of purpose.

Neither will entrance be denied to all such as love truly the unspeakable beauty of purity of life ; that is your password—purity.

Each soul will return along its own particular line or path towards the great future of perfection, and every life will have to be rendered strict account of in the final summing-up at the close of each life. That is the real day of judgment. It is a fact, not a fancy ; it is a day to be faced by each soul when its special moment has arrived, and justice will be shown to all, and then the soul will rest awhile before starting its life with us.

It may not reincarnate until it has definitely made up that which your people call the mind, to become enmeshed into fleshly bodies to fulfil the obligations incurred by it in the past, or to get a further chance of progress towards its heavenly goal.

Not all who deliberately seek poverty and distress are necessarily highly evolved in soul-structure, for, as your mind already knows, the vast majority of people are just in those poor suppressed conditions ; yet there is a certain class of soul of higher evolution which knows it must evolve certain life experiences through poverty, sickness, or even criminal conditions.

These souls need this very cruel testing to make them understand the very lowest type of human beings, and they will often make very fine leaders because a certain incarnation has given them insight into the workings of the minds of poor folk.

This is a very great step towards the end of physical evolution on your dense earth, if this particular soul makes good and succeeds in rising to great heights as some do.

The vast majority of poor, illiterate, or undeveloped races are really the most recently evolved soul-entities, and not in any way to be confused with specially individualized souls.

When very many poor souls are released from the great mass of soul-entities they must be immersed quickly into the waiting physical forms, and of course they fall into incarnation without much discrimination.

As they evolve, love makes them develop family or clan love, and by degrees a link is established between several souls of the same period of incubation, as it were, and these are born together as time goes on, and they become much more spiritual.

With regard to other souls which may elect to be born into families with whom they have no real soul kinship, they are often new to those families, and nothing draws them together. But yet this alien experience has its very special uses which is known to the soul before incarnation has even taken place in the body of the newly-born child.

Q. Did man evolve from and through the animal, and was he originally hermaphrodite, or was man an entirely separate evolution, and were the " Divine sparks " from God in etherical bodies evolving upward, to start their evolution at its appointed time on each of the spheres of gross matter ?

A. All Divine sparks evolved originally from soul material.

When we write about soul essence or soul material, we mean that part of infinity which is really unknowable in its beginning, for how can we or you really imagine a vast world beginning as a mere speck in a much vaster universe ?

We are all far too puny to begin to believe or even to be

able to imagine what the beginning really could have been in anything approaching idea in a concrete form.

Your ideas about evolution are very incorrect even as we ourselves know it, as your outlook is compelled at the present to be much limited by your lack of psychic development in the manner of sight.

It is as impossible to express correct details as to form as it is for a blind man to express colour and form in your own world. As we have remarked before, man is in no way descended from the monkeys. Man always had his own special place in evolution, and never in his own period of existence is there any trace of a legitimate descent through the monkey family.

One day your clever scientists will be absolutely convinced that there is no truth in this theory, but it dies hard.

The souls of men were only hermaphrodites in the immeasurably earliest possible period. Much that is in the " Book of Truth " is as allegorical as is the story in Genesis. No one teaching which can be regarded as absolutely correct can ever be given of a period so far back.

The Indian ideas about the breathing out of Brahma are in a measure allied to these, but they, too, recognize the allegory as such, and do not worry about these remote periods when time, as we know it now, did not exist.

The hermaphrodite was in effect the first individualized attempt to create some special entity which was in a measure a complete counterpart of God.

We want your minds to understand that Reincarnation is of mind or soul and spirit, so that there are really many layers, as it were, of incarnations to be worked out by each individual. Remember that we use the word " incarnation " because there is not another word which conveys just what we want your minds to understand in the fullest sense.

Mind and spirit take on certain forms, we mean what your minds would call a body, and then incarnation means the being enticed into or contained in a form or body, but not necessarily or entirely fleshly bodies.[1]

[1] A later note gave these words from the same Guide : " There is no incarnation of the same body, that is a term quite impossible. Incarnation of the soul in a variety of carnal bodies, and also *incarceration of the spiritual ego in a soul-body*, through æons of time and in many planetary bodies."

Matter is not exactly divisible, it interpenetrates in varying degrees of density, so that a body, as your minds call the physical envelope, may be at one type of incarnation, the soul-body at another period, and the spirit at yet another. Yet are they not three bodies, or three beings, or three entities, but one individualized being—man.

Now, when a soul is desirous of testing certain experiences, it will incarnate on your earth plane under the most suitable conditions for that test, not necessarily the happiest or most prosperous; but for some men these conditions prove too hard, and the soul retires somewhat baffled, and must return yet again and again until the test has been passed.

A soul lives many lives, or, more correctly, goes through many more individualized lives or periods of experience when divested of its fleshly envelope, and when it returns to your earth plane it is already an advance on its last expression of manhood.

Now, when the soul has passed its fullest number of tests bravely and wisely, then comes the time when it has earned release from physical life.

Then it receives the reward or distinguishing mark of what your scriptures call a white stone, a new name, a soul that is ransomed, as your church teaches, and it returns to go out no more.

This is only possible on its own individual merits, never by vicarious suffering on the part of a world Saviour.

The incarnation of the spirit cannot be entered into very extensively; it would need powers of communicating beyond the present understanding of human minds.

Q. Are we never really wholly and entirely " ourselves " during physical incarnation ?

A. No, not entirely, the person known by yourself and to your friends is not really the whole being as known even to us. Your other body is very beautiful indeed, as are all well-advanced souls, yet you suffer from fleshly disabilities, your faults are still part of your mind or soul, and your character is still beset by frailties, and yet your Self is full of wisdom, strength, and beauty.

The faults of the flesh which preclude man from the enjoyment of true spiritual contact are impurity of thought, speech, and actions; cruelty, spitefulness, malice, and all such things as hurt man's brotherhood.

God is Purity, God is Love, and only those whose hearts are pure and who love can contact the higher spiritual forces.

Now for a few moments let us try to consider this vexed question of man's right to know of his own past incarnations.

Your friends desire to be told of their own past incarnations. Well, why not ? As they say, it could not do harm, it might even help them to avoid errors in their present lives. Truly there is sense in this, and yet it is given to very few to lift the veil of their own past lives.

The reason is really a very simple one : it is a question of the faulty instruments at their disposal.

The brain is the chief storehouse or power station for storing mental pictures, but it is only a temporary building, as it were, nothing permanent.

So long as your people only use their brains (and many do not even use these humble tools) so long will pictures of long-forgotten pasts remain unrevealed, and their only knowledge will remain in certain instincts or vague memories.

Where the real soul or mind functions fully on the higher dimensions, there these pictures will be found very carefully stored up, and each will know his past existences, just as we know them for him.

Remember that even many who have passed beyond your present vision are not yet sufficiently advanced over here to be aware of these extended memories.

There are many, nay, many more divisions or grades of development on these other planes than with your own planet.

Sometimes knowledge is sent to your present brain for certain reasons, to explain certain facts in your present life, or for some special reason of assistance, as it may be the means of comfort or special understanding, but to the great mass such information, though available, is not given indiscriminately.

There is another aspect of incarnation never yet touched upon in the teachings on this subject, and that is the aspect of what one must term the higher degree of consciousness, a degree which allows man's soul to work its own incarnation independently of a man's body for the time being. It is a fact that the soul has a separate existence at all times, and can function quite independently of what yourselves would call your personality.

This is a limitation not heeded by the soul, and when at moments your mind feels the terrible cramp of your physical body then remember that your soul-body is fighting for a freedom unobtainable for the period destined for that particular inclusion in the physical body.

Such desires, such longings, such aspirations as perplex and torture the soul are the pangs of a cramped body spiritual, and a mind sore hindered in its expression of the inherent higher qualities of divine life. Self-expression is, indeed, the great need for every human being, and that is the only thing which will satisfy the awakening self-consciousness of each individual.

Tell this to your fellow beings. Let them understand what the cravings really mean.

Help all you meet to try to understand what they think is self-expression. For what is this divine unrest? this desire to create? to make, to bring forth out of a submerged soul a definite created thing? However mean, humble, however great and glorious in conception, so long as it is sincere, and so long as the best of a man's heart is given to make it, produce or create it, this is in truth man's puny attempt to follow his heaven-born instincts to create, or procreate, to emulate God whose image he was and is intended to be.

Art, music, drama, literature, poetry, all are splendid ends towards a great goal. Handicrafts, producing flowers, machines, even furniture, designing of all kinds, whether in colour-form or vibratory contrivances, all these are the signs of a live soul-effort towards self-expression in creation.

Yes, indeed, the soul leads a much larger life on other planes of existence ; and in sleep, unconsciousness, severe illness bringing unconsciousness, trance states, all these absent moments release the soul temporarily for its larger life, and most unwillingly some of them return to earth conditions.

The less evolved soul has also at moments unsatisfied longings which a poor, weak, or coarse physical body will seek to help in evil ways, hence vice, drink, sensuality. That is why transmutation is a wiser doctrine to teach than suppression.

This will one day be the acknowledged cure for crime—but not yet.

Q.   What is the reason of decadence ?

A.   Decadence is a very curious disease of the soul and must always be arrested in its growth, for it is a poisonous fungus of quick growth, insidious, hateful, and dangerous to the community in general.   It precedes racial decline.

Always point out to those who plead for a better understanding, that there is a very wide gulf between truth as the decadent would establish it, and truth as the purist would have it.

One is of the devil, of forces evil, retrogressive, dangerous, and entangled with the lower occultism as we see it here.

There is no extenuation for those unhappy decadents, they have deliberately chosen evil instead of good, and nothing save the most unhappy working out of their sins can ever save their souls and spiritual entities.

CHAPTER XXII

REINCARNATION (*contd.*)

Age of Souls. Space. The Individualised Spirit. Spirit Communication. Development of Talents. Antagonism. The Reincarnating Form. Balance of Sexes. Affinities. The Reincarnating Fragment. Life on other Planets. Is Reincarnation Speedy? Reincarnation of Pet Animals. Karma. Justice or Mercy? Compensation.

REINCARNATION.

Q. Are all born into this world for the first time at the same state of soul development?

A. Your souls are all at different stages of development because they pass into your present human bodies at very different periods of your own earth history.

Please remember that life on your earth is of very ancient origin.[1]

We watch your childish attempts to approach this stupendous subject with amusement.

Must your minds really insist on a beginning, they must go back beyond sentient life on your planet, because soul material is far older than physical material—indeed souls vary in age, of course they do, just as trees or any of the common things around yourselves.

Q. Can you tell us how it is that we are compelled to speak of young souls and old souls?

A. Your ideas of young souls and old souls are perfectly correct, the difference is really a matter of number of incarnations and of the advance made by each individualized soul during the period of each incarnation on earth.

But your souls sometimes incarnate in between long periods on other planes of existence. Planes more advanced, too, so that when they return to your earth plane they are older in wisdom and understanding.

---

[1] See *Constitution of Man*, p. 130.

Q. Have there been different outpourings of individual-ized souls as the Theosophists teach ?

A. Yes, they are quite correct in this. The Great Logos, as they call the Being at the beginning of creation, sent down great waves as it were of soul material, which hitting space, split into small particles at very widely divergent times of Cosmic history. This was before the individualizing period mentioned in the " Book of Truth."

It is, of course, perfectly true that God was not able to withhold this splitting up of many sparks of divine or Cosmic energy, because even then there was free will on the part of individualization; but there were æons of time between each wave, and the real differences of soul development depend on individual effort.

The Logos pours out His divine energy from time to time, when fresh souls are to be incarnated. Men require renewal, as so many pass on in time to other systems and their places must be filled by younger souls.

Whenever there is a need for them God is always ready to send out fresh souls; they are always immature, but they keep His special gift of free will, the only part of His creation with this special gift, and very much abused and misunderstood it is.

Q. " Great waves of soul material which ' hitting space ' split." Can you explain this further ?

A. Your ideas of space are not very clear, for space to us is the body or material of a coarser fibre which was the rock, as it were, on which the soul-essence was poured out, and as it fell—(but remember, all these terms are incorrect in their primary meaning)—but when the soul-essence was flung out, or down, or on, or through, it hit the receiving atmosphere or material, of the kind which densified into forms later on. The essence was really rather like shot being poured from a great height in a fluid form and making round forms on hitting the water-tanks below.

Q. Is it the same individualized spirit which reincarnates each time ?

A. The individualized spirit makes its appearance with each fleshly incarnation as most people believe, but the individualized spirit also makes many incarnations in the interim between one physical incarnation and another in the higher of the soul's existences on other planes of matter. When a soul leaves the body it makes a journey to the plane which attracts it by force of vibration, and when it is established in special work there, it continues through a multitude of experiences until some attraction calls it back to an earth body. This attraction is usually through a re-entry into physical form of a debtor or of some great lover, or because of a special opportunity of work to be performed ; back flies the soul-body into outer or physical manifestations, to work on until the next holiday from coarser or harsher experiences has been earned. This goes on æon after æon until final release has been earned.

Q. When a person is no longer on the earth plane and is received on a higher plane than usual, can that soul enter again into communication with those it has left behind ?

A. As a general rule there is never any real break in communication at all, but when a soul is very highly evolved, it has such much more important work to do that it has no special call to return to your earth plane. There is no real need because in a curious way contact is always possible when those on the earth plane are in the state of sleep or trance ; it is always soul-contact, remember.

Q. If persons start any work—such as music or painting, etc., in a desultory manner on this earth, are they bound to bring it to full completion on the other plane before re-incarnating here again ?

A. Yes, this is in a measure true, but not entirely so. When a soul is in favour of developing certain gifts, or going through certain experiences, the soul may only attain a very desultory knowledge of these tastes or faculties of expression in this particular life. That starts a certain vibration, which, once started, will continue to vibrate until it attains the complete note or sound in other lives, or on other planes of existence. It is not so hopeless as your friend appears to think, it will only lead to a further education of vibratory force.

Q. Why is there sometimes antagonism between mother and child ? Is it to work off a debt ?

A. This question of antagonism is, of course, most difficult to understand unless the enquirer understands all that reincarnation means to the individual. Never does antagonism exist unless there is a serious debt in the past between those two souls, an antagonism which many incarnations may have to wipe away.

Q.   Do we after death keep the forms of our previous incarnation until we reincarnate ?   What happens to these forms when we reincarnate ?

A.   Your own forms must always be retained as marks of recognition or personality ; but form is not really what your own minds mean by form ; it retains auric form ; that is to say the character must go on from form to form although it remains the same in essential points.   Remember, sex is nothing, merely some material form of outward expression.   The soul is not male or female as your minds know these terms.   But when a soul assumes its separate life, it assumes a power which is positive or male, or negative or female.   Each soul works in couples, that is why your minds, much more intuitive than your own thoughts understand, are conscious of affinities.   These affinities work together in various ways, sometimes as man and woman, sometimes as mother and child, sometimes as friends ; sometimes they divide, one here with us, one there with your own much troubled and unhappy body, for there is never complete happiness of soul when affinities are divided by life, or by that which your minds erroneously call death.   Now when an affinity is here, then the great demand for reunion brings about a very strong psychic development which is used by Guides for much useful information to be made public.

Q.   If affinities reincarnate at the same time on earth are they bound to meet ?

A.   No.

Q.   Does the soul also choose the sex of the body in which it reincarnates ?   If so, how is the numerical balance between the men and women maintained ?

A.   The soul must always decide the sex, for there are certain experiences to be gained through each sex, but the question of numerical balance is not very vital really, because there are always souls which make constant journeys between your two worlds.   We mean that there is not the same need for human sex distinction to be maintained in the earth.   At the same time numbers vary and it would

be inaccurate to say the equilibrium is strictly maintained
on your earth, there is true equilibrium of souls, not necessarily in your earthly form however.

Q. Are the male and female principles always separate
from the beginning ? Are they always in pairs and do
these pairs constitute affinities ?

A. The souls are always in pairs in the human evolution.
They assume the differences known to your physical sight
on manifestation in their physical forms ; they never
unite again until the great Day of Union on the higher
planes, and then it is not union but the intermingling of two
entities that will never be quite the same again, for the
souls have a very prolonged life on all planes of existence
so that the affinities meet and have long periods of happiness
together in many realms or spheres of existence. This
division of the original soul-sparks into two individual
forces is a very vast and very far-reaching cosmic event,
and it is not possible for any minds yet clothed in human
bodies to realize the real end of cosmic events.

Q. What part of the last form comes into the infant ?

A. Your soul returns to a very small collection of material
atoms, a mould is prepared for it. The soul wishes to be
re-born and because certain experiences are necessary to
its further development, a number of atoms is made to
collect into a material nucleus as it were, which is
made into the form by the ovum in the womb of the
intended mother. This then is the form which is to be
the new outward expression of your own soul, your soul
remains the same ; the soul is always the same, it never
changes except in its outward form, but not form as your
minds call it.

Your ideas are much influenced by that sense which is
given through your eyes. Form is the idea of God made
into a series of vibratory developments, which is the secret
of the idea of the immanence of God in all things. The
infant is only a collection of atoms at best, and the soul is
the soul apart all the time, and leading a far wider, greater
individual life unknown to any outward expression at all.
Matter or dense physical form is not your great soul
at all, it is only a minute portion of a very great whole ;
a whole unknown in its grandeur by your finite minds
after all.

This question of souls and their reincarnations is very difficult, for it is not the whole soul-body which reincarnates at all, but only a very small portion of it, that is to say, at present there is only a remnant of your great soul inhabiting each of your present bodies. The more advanced the soul the more exclusively is it employed in other realms of existence, only a very limited part lives in your present bodies. We all move together in another dimension simultaneously with your present portion of earth-bound souls, which are often conscious of terribly cramped conditions. Your real permanent soul-bodies are very much greater than your physical brains can understand and lead totally different lives with us ; that is why we are able to communicate at all times with your own physical brain ; your soul is really living in our presence all the while, there is not any real separation but only at a certain stage of advancement can your minds really become aware of this ; that is why clairvoyance, clairaudience, and the fourth dimension are perfectly possible and very natural features of your enlarged consciousness.

Q. Is this major portion of our soul cognizant of what the minor soul is doing ? Or is it indifferent ?

A. Yes, the major part, as your brains call it, is always conscious of the minor portion. It is, of course, the Self, and the self, your own small self is only a very insignificant part of the greater Self.

Q. Must a human soul reincarnate until it has been through all its initiations ?

A. This is a very difficult question to answer, as life on your earth plane may change for life on another planetary body, with still a material body to work in. We cannot always see what will be the end of every man's incarnation, using this world as your place of material bodies ; there are many others, and your lives cross over to other starry bodies or planets. Your earth makes contact in ether with others and your races send people across from time to time, but spiritually life must end in these higher states of much more highly evolved consciousness.

Q. Is it permitted to ask the earth names of the planets with which we exchange incarnations ?

A. Do not ask this question ; for names known to your own people do not exist outside your own world, and the planets which your people visit are unnamed in your own scheme of planets. The names we give would not convey anything to your minds at all ; suffice it to say that there are planets to which your souls come and on which many lives are often spent, all for a very good and divine purpose, but we must say nothing more. The earth as we see it is the lowest or densest type of planet used for your own souls.

Q. When any dearly-loved persons pass over do they reincarnate on this earth during the current lifetime of their particular relatives ?

A. No, of course not, they all need rest and refreshment, also further experience of life over here. We are only given certain types of souls which visit certain spheres ; these may return as Guides, perhaps rather as their spirit advisers, in much closer relationship than even earthly companionship makes possible. Life must be lived out fully over here, also without the physical hindrances which impede the soul's progress, and when the time comes for return it will be in a much more advanced state. There are many degrees of experience to be lived through out of the physical body, even by the more advanced soul ; and we must always let the soul choose its own incarnation of its own accord.

Others who come are backward, they need teaching, and must often return to very bad conditions ; these must, of course, rest over here first for a longer spell than is usually the case with the very highly evolved soul. For the highly evolved soul is, as a rule, in a hurry to conclude his turn of physical lives to carry out his higher destiny.

When a soul has very important work to finish it may return very speedily to finish it, not so speedily as a few years, of course, but a century or so would be quite possible.

Q. What becomes of pet animals ? Do they not develop into souls via group souls ? (Comp. Theos. teaching.)

A. Not souls as you understand them, but they do reincarnate if their love is strong for some one in the past.[1]

Q. Will you give us instruction in the law of Karma ?

A. This very interesting point is very closely linked up

[1] See p. 45.

with the truth of such subjects as reincarnation, forgiveness of sins, punishment, and all such kindred subjects.

Much will be understood if your minds once grasp the truth that whatsoever a man sows that shall the man reap sooner or later ; if not in this present life then in a future ; not necessarily on the earth plane, for Karma is worked out within all planes of existence, not only through your earthly bodies. Without doubt, what is done by any living human being is wiped out or rewarded somewhere, somehow, and there can be no readjusting which allows one jot or one tittle to be removed from that man's own tale of credit or of discredit.

Responsibility is a very little recognized law of judgment, that is judgment by your God, Master, or the Heavenly Father as your minds prefer to call the Great Being in charge of your particular evolution on the present earth plane.

We know that much harm has been done by the strange irresponsible teaching of the washing away of sin by Him whom your hearts know as Jesus the Christ. My children, this same Jesus Christ may long to shield and help much suffering entailed by man's own folly, and He is ever ready to guide, or advise, or even to help those who are sinned against, to show mercy towards those who offend against love, mercy, and justice, but such is the law of the Universe that even He cannot avert what is due to a man for evil ; nor must He, for only so can justice be done and law maintained in your planet.

Now, with regard to some of the laws which rule your planet, there is a very fine law, the law of compensation, or shall we call it by its better name, the law of spiritual equilibrium, a law of balance, and a law never allowed to, indeed it cannot, deviate from a very mathematically correct standard. Compensation is found throughout Nature, it is in evidence everywhere, in places little suspected, amongst people who apparently have nothing to give them hope or pleasure, but yet in their inner senses some anodyne is prepared and administered ; unless as in such cases as a speeding-up of punishment for former ill-doing, they appear to be most heavily afflicted, yet should they rejoice, for God sees fit to wipe out errors of the past in a more drastic fashion to speed-up their soul's development.

Q. I do not understand the " law of compensation, or spiritual equilibrium "—it would appear to involve the principle of mercy, whereas the law of Karma is strict justice.

A. That is a very excellent question, for it involves a very much misunderstood law of the Great Heavenly Father.

Your soul revolts at the idea of strict justice, being far more inclined towards mercy as your own scriptures teach it, and very rightly. Yet though each individual should practise mercy towards all his fellow-beings, it will be strict justice that is received from his Heavenly Father. Know this, my children, there can be no shirking of individual responsibility for aught that is ill-done to your fellow men, nor any failure in the receipt of reward for that which is well and faithfully done ; all is carried out to the letter, and only by a strict carrying out of this first law of equilibrium may the law of balance be kept, and that is most important.

But there is a method of helping each other over the rough places which self-indulgence or folly has created, and that is by the merciful attitude of a sympathetic mind towards all those who should justly suffer by those whose sufferings might condemn these ill-doers. That is the real necessity of forgiveness as in your own Lord's Prayer, but there is always a proper balancing out of good for good, evil for evil.

Q. You spoke at a circle of an " anodyne " which is prepared for those who appear to be placed in very bad circumstances. Will you explain this more ?

A. Yes, that is very true. Nature has a very marvellous method of adjusting what on the surface appears to be very ill, and which might give very unhappy lives indeed, as among the poor, the blind, the mentally afflicted and so forth ; but as a general rule these other people amongst the poor and uneducated are less sensitive to outer conditions than are those who are much more highly developed. It is a fact that a highly trained (or over-trained) mind is something rather more difficult to rule or influence than a rough or untutored one ; a highly bred animal is more difficult to train or to rear than a common kind ; a child of sensitive parents is more difficult to rear than one of peasant folk.

N

This is common knowledge, all these are Nature's compensations, as your minds can easily understand, but in the case of those souls who have deliberately chosen poor or deformed bodies there is no outward joy or compensation, only in the greater soul, that is not seen or even believed in, there is a feeling of satisfaction that at last the chance comes to pay a bad debt.

CHAPTER XXIII

MYSTERY SCHOOLS

Introduction by M.B. February 27th. The White Brotherhood resumes.
Loss of Christian Mysteries. Æsthetic Training. The Goal of Mystery
Teaching. Qualifications Required. Man Made Perfect. Need for
Mystery Schools.

NOTE.—*The introductory part of this chapter was written by myself in
obedience to the reiterated wish of the Guides.*—M.B.

"Behold I show you a mystery. We shall all be changed."
"He that hath ears to hear let him hear."

THE two outstanding Teachers in the New Testament,
which purports to be the Sacred Book on which the whole
conception of Christianity rests, are Jesus the Christ and
Paul.

It is significant that both these Teachers speak quite
definitely of a more advanced code or method of training
the human soul which is quite apart from and which apparently is quite definitely intended to transcend the ordinary
everyday teaching for the ordinary man.

The "other things" which were deferred by Jesus until
such time as the disciples were fit to receive subtler and
more mystical teaching can only refer to such inner teaching
which was given a little at a time until the spiritual intelligences of His hearers had sufficiently awakened to perceive
the powers which lay behind their Master, powers which He
definitely promised should be passed on to all those whose
development reached the necessary standard of knowledge.

None can read the teaching given by Jesus in all the
Gospel narratives, and more particularly that given through
the mediumship of John the Mystic, without some kind of
acknowledgment that the teaching, as Jesus the Christ gave
it out, is far above the ordinary understanding of the
ignorant, although at the same time the ignorant may find

therein a code of spiritual living, simple and compatible with ordinary everyday life.

There is a way, a truth, a life indicated which can only be followed by such as have reached a certain period in their souls' evolution that enables them to take up the Cross, to forsake the World, to renounce all that a man hath in order to seek *first* the Kingdom of Heaven : such are marks of definite spiritual longing which set certain types of soul apart from their fellows.

It is the failure to take note of this definite line of demarcation in the soul's individualized pilgrimage which has left Christianity in a state of stupor, of slackness, lacking vision or desire of attainment.

In vain at the present day do we bemoan the failure of Churches, creeds, dogmas : in vain bewail the indifference of modern youth to all religious exercise or desire for religious guidance.

For centuries, indeed from its foundation, the exponents of the Christian Revelation have forgotten the meaning of the word and have led their unhappy followers into blind alleys of dogma, content themselves with their own narrow reading of the letter of the Christian concept, ignorant of the stultifying effect of these limitations on the more thoughtful and striving of those whom they set out to teach.

Now, just so surely as we know that that which is the ideal of happiness, beauty, recreation, enjoyment of one type of human being, may quite conceivably be diametrically opposed to that which expresses these same emotions to another type, so in common sense must we recognize that the souls of different types are of different grades of development and demand certain defined degrees of spiritual knowledge before each striving soul can be really satisfied.

It is true that each may find the truth for himself, yet it is amazingly difficult where faith is hardly established, where vision barely awakened, and the urge of the spirit only dimly sensed in a vague feeling of the uncertainty of a future life, an uneasiness of mind that does not know quite what to believe or what doctrine to accept, to step out from the common rut of the unthinking sheep-like mass with the definite resolution : " I will arise."

Yet human nature has always been the same, and being

the same, the soul of its own volition turns towards a goal unseen and unsuspected in the crowded, impermanent turmoil of life as we know it here and now.

Modern discoveries, modern thought, modern outlook, modern art, music, drama, modern and more universal education, however much we may decry or belittle all these, leave their mark on the mind and heart of each individual to-day.

We may flatter ourselves that the effect is superficial, and so it is in a way, but we are not exaggerating our case when we say that although we are aware of the fact through research into antiquity that civilizations have existed which are now lost, but which at one time must have been as fine and as progressive as our own, we have also to remember that the law of the Cosmos brings each wave of civilization a little further than the last, and that as each crest advances that little further, so as each recedes, the level never sinks quite so low as the preceding one.

Each civilization has had its own great religious teaching. God has never hidden His face from any of His children. The nobler the civilization, the conception of God becomes correspondingly noble. The downfall of the civilization has been due to the corruption of power, the arrogance of the priesthood, or the effect of a natural cataclysm, of which it is now impossible to gauge the immensity.

But considering only such comparatively modern civilizations as the ancient Chaldeans, Aryan, Egyptian, Greek or Roman (for modern they are when we remember the age of the earth), we are always confronted with the story of a mystical side to the popular or generally accepted religion of the time.

No age was without its recognition of God and no religion was without its school of inner teaching for the more educated or more deeply thinking minds.

Fortunately our libraries and museums afford us written, inscribed, or tabular witness of these facts.

Can we seriously believe, then, that in the most recent of all religious revelations for the aspiring and educated mind, for the longing, loving spirit of man, there is no such inner mystical teaching, and that the bare outline of Christianity such as we receive in the churches and chapels of to-day is all that is necessary to each, whatever his degree of mental equipment ? Or that there exists no key to much that is mysterious and incomprehensible in the scriptures when we search them diligently in the privacy of our own hearts ?

M. B.

June, 1928.

.   .   .   .   .   .

At this point this subject was changed, and not referred to again until February 27, 1929, when quite unexpectedly it was resumed. Additional matter was given on March 7th, March 25th (when the title of the book was given), and the concluding paper was received on July 1st.

FEBRUARY 27, 1929.

We wish to tell you some interesting points on the subject of the ancient mystery schools, for, of course, very little survives your present-day knowledge of the mystical and spiritual centres of true religious understanding.

Know then, that although much is talked about the need for esoteric teaching in the world to-day, there is, as a matter of fact, much teaching in existence which is on the true lines of mysticism, only it is not easily discovered.

There is a tendency to hide too much wisdom teaching like veritable needles in bundles of straw, and those who would benefit very much by a light being thrown on their darkness are left to continue their ways in darkness ; it is not really the way to help on spiritual evolution.

We wish this book to throw just such a light, and we shall proceed to give out teaching which will show up these particular schools of thought, so that each individual may choose for himself the method best suited to his own temperament.

With regard to the very foolish idea that there is no more mystical teaching behind the church teaching than is given openly in the gospel fragments as now extant, that is very stupid, and only shows how ignorant the priests and ministers of this most mystical religion are in the conception of the life and doctrine of the Great Being whose servants they aspire to be ; for Christ not only partook of the esoteric schools' doctrine of his own time, the Essenes

and the Therapeutæ, but He amalgamated the best ideas
out of both these schools into a school of further revelation
Himself, and taught a very advanced form of spiritual
alchemy or understanding of laws of the very beginnings of
things, and tried to explain to His more advanced followers
what was the real destiny of the Human Man who attained
perfection and ultimate godhead, as, of course, this is the
real goal of Man made perfect, the actual stature of the
extreme Christ-consciousness, the ultimate end of all
mankind.

This at first appears totally impossible of fulfilment, but
one must always remember that man was originally a
divinity before blind forces set him plunging ever downwards
into denser and yet denser matter, which results in Man as
your minds know him now, longing for some thing, some end,
some aim half forgotten, entirely, unbelievably great, a
longing which fills all his many lives, so that he passes from
life to life in a continual search for that which is lost, the
eternal quest for God within his own heart, the real Godhead
which is now dimly, vaguely, yet ever more and more
definitely unveiled to Man's astonished gaze as he con-
templates immanent God, immanent divinity, immanent
wisdom and love in all manifested life, whether of the physical
forms known to your own outward sense of sight, or whether
known to a further and yet more glorious contemplation of
Beauty hidden within the fourth dimension.

Divinity abounds everywhere, and may be discovered in
all places by those who have faith and by those whose
innate sense of beauty makes them aware of values un-
dreamed of by their ordinary fellow-beings.

This is the value of æsthetic training, this is the need for
an understanding of those ancient teachers, the Greeks,
whose ideas of beauty, expressed in outward simplicity, can
never be overestimated.

Do not be misled into thinking too little of what youth
calls academic ; do not be led into ugliness of expression,
because certain types are being tinged with what youth
chooses to call realism.

Beauty is perfection in detail. Take any of the tiniest
work of those beings not even believed in by the majority
of your own people, the Nature spirits, who design the
smallest detail of flowers. How perfect in every part, in form,

colour of petal, in perfume of body. Yet these colours and forms and perfumes are as nothing, if your eyes could only see the beauty of their *types*, as conceived by their Devas on the inner planes of matter.

Now, of course, these are rather beside the points we were considering, and yet when one tries to tell the people of what the immanence of Godhead or of divinity really means, it is truly difficult to limit its expression to a few pages.

There is so very much to tell, so very much to increase the wonder of seeking man in the realms of Nature, that only by a contemplation of God-power in all the myriad forms of manifestation and expression can mankind be made aware of what his inheritance really is ; for remember the real object of man in his present life is to learn to take up again, not the cross of suffering, but the mystical cross of forces creative, redemptive, and, above all, mystically creative, and mystically able to rise into a degree of life beyond physical expression, such as was typified by the ascension into the higher state of Christ-consciousness.

Naturally such a wondrous vista is not for the man immersed in material enjoyment of physical prosperity ; so hardly shall a rich man enter the Kingdom of Heaven, said your Master. Truly the test of riches is very severe, for riches blind the soul to so much simple beauty, and all truth is simple and all beauty is truth in essence.

There is one very great necessity for the training of the man for the great adventure of the soul (this taking up of the Cross of Creation, the symbol of spirit raising matter to a very high spiritual degree), and that great need is the spirit of love and of faithfulness in the discharge of every obligation towards all those whose lives enter into touch with our own.

There is an obligation between man and man ; an obligation between man and ourselves, and we in turn have our own mighty obligations to the Great Beings whose powers are immeasurably above our own spiritual lights.

Life Cosmic is terribly complex, and we are all fearfully and wonderfully evolved out of primordial essences, and even in these high spheres there is much beyond our own comprehension.

How then can your puny minds expect to comprehend

the complete details of creation and such-like ? It is beyond our power to express it in a simple enough kind of language appropriate to the greatest intellects amongst your earth-bound people. The briefest outline is all that can be of service to your minds, minds which are staggered by a dimension as simple as the fourth.

The goal of all mystery teaching is, then, an attempt to train the physical man to sense his psychic faculties so that even dimly he may sense the path along which his soul must travel back to its own intelligence, to the many, many mansions of his Father's House.

MARCH 7, 1929.

The real use of mystery schools was, of course, to prepare the more advanced minds of the ancient days to contact the higher consciousness, for by special exercises and by intense self-culture they learnt much about their own individual relationship to the universal laws.

The prevailing ideas were founded on the close relation-ship of a man to the universe in general. This is a very important point because the very close similarities were part of his inherent knowledge, and the use of rhythmic breathing, curious forms of gesture, dance, words of power, all these tuned man's body, soul, and spirit into a very high degree of what your minds would call exaltation or ecstasy or mental intoxication—the state of mind in which a mentality was raised high above a merely physical sensory state to a very pure and exalted reaction to the Divine Light, or intuned to the Gnosis or Divine Wisdom.

The strictest purity, the highest degree of morality, the most perfect detachment from all earthly things, influences, or desires, was the sole recommendation. Mere intellectual growth, curiosity, or selfish desire for wisdom precluded any man from the right of initiation. Hence the very severe tests on all planes of matter before Man was really and conclusively admitted a fully qualified member of any school.

None was allowed to leave once he had taken the final vows of fidelity and of secrecy. If a man were found un-worthy, rather than allow him to betray, or even make little of these important secrets which had been entrusted to him, he was made to suffer some dire penalty which should render him speechless, or lifeless, or blind and incompetent, so that nothing was allowed to pass out into the outer world at all.

Such secrets as were vouchsafed to him in due gradation, as or when he had proved himself fit to be passed on through the closed portals, have never been disclosed to mankind now on earth ; they are too dangerous for merely human minds or brains, since through them Man is empowered to ally himself to forces vast and creative, forces which would render an unwise or unfaithful custodian a very real menace to his fellow-beings.

You will naturally have guessed by now the real importance of ancient freemasonry ; not the very innocuous tradition of this mystery teaching which survives in your midst at the present time. One day we will tell your world much more on this subject, but not yet.

These mystery schools were part of the ordinary religious life of the race which had been instructed in the type of teaching peculiarly suited to its constitution ; but, of course, all fundamental ideas rest on the same basis, a basis of belief in the divinity of Man, the immanence of a God-spirit in all planes of existence, and the final working out by Man of the individualized part of his own particular stature of perfection.

Naturally only the barest outlines of good conduct, upright dealing, brotherhood and so forth were talked about to the mass of people in general. They held that a man's soul remained unworthy of divine wisdom until a certain degree of education had been imparted to himself, and education was the right of those only who had been incarnated a certain number of times on the physical plane.

These beings were never allowed to receive instruction from the lesser of those who officiated, until they were able to give full proof of certain degrees of proficiency in the liberal arts and sciences, as your Masonry tells you even in your present rituals.

It was quite understood that religion was of very great importance to the soul's advancement, until later, a kind of bleak philosophy entirely mental in aspect attracted a particular type of human mind, and man was ruled by his own desire for the power which wisdom could give him, and not ruled by a burning, living love of his Creator and of his brother.

Such was the time when the Christian school of mystery was founded, and this was completely founded on a newer system of loving understanding of the sacred needs of mankind for the many assurances that the Great Being known as God really cared for His children.

Now, of course, from an outward point of view the teaching of Jesus, the Master of this newer school, was to all outward appearance a very simple one ; apparently there were no wonderful secrets of divine laws, no special places of meditation and prayer, no special ritualistic exercises. He merely taught the people to love one another, and He taught the selected few how to heal, apart from the usually accepted medical craft.

But all the way through the story of His life, His teaching points the way in symbol and allegory to a very real scheme of ritualistic proceedings meant to crystallize into a very definite school of mysticism. These symbols are perfectly recognizable to those whose minds are alive to the ancient language of symbols. Certain experiences were lived through and were allowed to be noted by His followers as they would have to consolidate all this into a properly constituted school when the time came. Had His method been fully carried out by those who survived His death, there would be now a very different state of affairs in your Christian Church, but words used symbolically were taken literally, acts of a ritualistic import were given a very mundane interpretation, and the Christian Creed became a system of error instead of a highly developed method of learning the truth in a world grown weary of outward observances and longing for inner guidance.

PURPORT OF MYSTERY TEACHING.

The aim, as we were remarking, of mystery teaching, is to establish a living connection between God the Father and each of His children in the human family.

All life is linked together in this marvellous scheme of the Heavenly Father, or the Great Overseer, or the Great Architect, whatever your hearts recognize as the Ruler of your own inner selves. The story of the prodigal son in your own scriptures is the story of the awakening soul, who, after living through all the coarser experiences of physical lives, suddenly becomes aware of a divine home-sickness as it were ; he arises and sets out on the long journey home to his Heavenly Father. His welcome is assured ; he will receive the ring, the garments and the feast of rejoicing.

Every soul is a prodigal son. Every soul must one day awake ; every soul will one day sigh for his Father's House. Oh ! do tell your own people how much the whole of creation depends for happiness on the individual awakening of each soul, and how much each soul can really accomplish by this setting-out towards the Father's House.

Your hearts are heavy when you behold the sickness, suffering, and misery of your fellow-beings ; but your hearts must learn that no effort to raise the eyes above, no sigh for their own home, no striving for their higher selves is ever wasted in the sum of human lives in the mass. The greater the number of these who definitely seek God as the goal of their desires, the quicker will the raising of the whole scale of human evolution become in vibration. By slow degrees your individual influence steals into the hearts and minds of those with whom your daily life is lived. Light shines into dark recesses, healing covers the secret wounds of bodies and souls ; life is poured into empty vessels, standards of spirituality are raised, the first streaks of dawn glimmer across the murky sky, a soft breath pervades the heated cities of millions of fretful and busy folk ; —all eyes turn towards the Father's House, and the vast pilgrimage of human evolution starts afresh towards the unseen promised land.

Herein lie the object, then, of preparing a band of those who can teach, write, heal, and love their fellow-beings. Herein lie our own present need and the need we have of mediums who will definitely say to all within their auras (for remember that the extent of a man's aura is the extent of his sympathy)—" We have something to tell your hearts about the real joy of living for one another, we can show your minds this unsuspected path in your very midst, we can tell your souls that the great Brotherhood of MAN MADE PERFECT is the guiding Brotherhood behind all your movements towards life eternal, towards understanding, towards the most Christlike endeavours of all who confess and call themselves Christians." (At the end of this paragraph my hand was made to return and underline heavily the words " Man Made Perfect.")

Yes, that is to be the title of this mystical book.

Q. Then the whole title is to be " Man Made Perfect : the Science of Spiritual Evolution " ?

A. Yes, at last we have got through this very important fact, the great title.

We wish to give a further instruction on this subject of Mystery Schools, as it is necessary to make our readers understand that there was a very real need for such schools in the past, and that there will always be a need for secret instruction on Mystery Teaching suited to the soul more spiritually advanced in its pilgrimage Home.

Know then, my children, that the real need for the establishment of such schools of further teaching lies in the fact which is shown in the subject of reincarnation— that souls are of very varied degrees of development, and that just as a young child must attend a kindergarten, as your own people call it, so the younger souls need only the rudiments of training, the work being to train and mould the character in the way of love and self-control, of service, and of all honourable dealing with their fellow-beings.

When the soul has accomplished these earlier lessons, then the time approaches for its admission into a school where individual thought, individual desire, and individual search after wisdom must be satisfied and encouraged.

Such admission was accorded by your ancient schools of Mysticism, when the intellect was truly awakened, the heart pure, the body sound, and the whole man desirous of becoming better acquainted with the object of his own creation, with his own part in the system of universal creation, and with his intuition, awakened to the unseen but realized planes of existence with which he felt himself surrounded.

In those earlier days, before the grosser materialism, which is so prevalent amongst your own people to-day, had entirely swamped the feeling of unseen planes, and before the knowledge of contacting unseen forces had been lost to the more gifted spiritual leaders of mankind, there was a fully recognized system of training, and certain powers of the magnetic and etheric bodies were recognized and stimulated by prescribed methods ; so that, before a man passed out of his physical body, he had already great power and knowledge which enabled him to pass beyond, in a state of a more highly evolved condition than is usually the case in these days on your earth.

We have already told you how certain expressions, methods, signs, words, and customs, in your present Masonic ritual are dim shadows of actual soul experiences in the past mysteries, and every person who is a Mason can follow all this information very clearly for himself ; we need only remind the reader that what is now a pictorial representation of spiritual events or experiences, was, at one time, a very true experience that left its mark on the candidate for each degree of initiation into still loftier degrees of consciousness.

The day has yet to dawn when these mysteries have to be restored, but this will not be yet, not until the present differences in the great principles underlying these mysteries are broken up, disintegrated, and the entrance into these mysteries as true members is not proscribed by sex, but is a matter of the loftiness of the soul, the desire for union with the Heavenly Initiator, and the wonderful ideal of the brotherhood of souls in the higher meaning of the word.

It is at this point that one must consider how this idea of a setting apart of certain members of the Christian religion was emphasised by its Founder—Jesus the Christ— for no great religion is without this inner side ; this is a well known fact, as your own remarks have already shown, and because of this ignorant setting aside of the very words of this mighty Founder, so has the Christian religion failed to hold the more intellectually minded, the more enquiring amongst your church people to-day.

The mystery side is not lacking, but the real teachers of this mystery side are lacking, and the people are as sheep having no shepherd, for the shepherds are, for the most part, hirelings.

However, the day approaches when the hirelings shall be found out, and the true spiritual leaders will once more lead the sheep beside the still waters of spiritual knowledge.

There are actually in existence, in your own midst, written evidences of these inner teachings, as left by the Great Hierophant and Initiator—Jesus the Christ ; but the dust of ages covers them yet, and they are not known to your times ; but they will be found, and much will be changed in years to come in the outlook of Christian peoples all over the world.

Meanwhile, in the heart of each man, there still glimmers the small flame of divinity, waiting to be fanned into a refiner's fire, which shall consume away all ignorance, all dross, all bigotry, all self-seeking, making of each man a torch for the mysteries of the Kingdom of God.

Think on these things.

CHAPTER XXIV

INITIATION

A Real Experience. The Loss to the Physical World. The Ritual. The Soul's Awakening. The Way of Service. The Way of Contemplation. The Way of Renunciation. The Way of Healing.

THE subject of Initiation is one which deals with matters of such a very high mystical import, that very seldom is it possible to allow this information to be sent into the materialistic world, which is entirely unaware that this adventure of the soul is open to all who seek this mystic quest, and that to-day, no less than many centuries ago, there is a way, a truth and a life of the soul, which may be sought and entered upon during the present physical life on earth.

In our instruction on the Mystery Schools, we have mentioned this quest, and told the reader that just as this adventure was sought by the ancient Egyptian and Greek, so may it be sought, encountered, and undertaken to-day in your own midst by all such as desire the things of the spirit, rather than the fleshpots of material enjoyment.

This soul's adventure is undertaken already by many who feel that life is only a fragment of a very big career, and we who long to welcome each soul on its path toward God the Great Initiator, we desire to place on record through this woman, who is our medium, a definite teaching for all to read whom it may concern, that not only do these mysteries exist, they are actually part of your spiritual home-life with us.

In schools of secret teaching, in occult brotherhoods, this fact is known and realized, but we send this message out into your midst—there is a home of spiritual beauty far beyond all earthly imaginings, wherein the soul may seek asylum from the frets of worldly existence, where rule the Great Masters, Teachers, and Hierophants, of all evolutions and of all civilizations.

These perfected Men, who once lived in your midst, are now your helpers in your struggles towards that measure of perfection advocated and taught by the Blessed Master and Chief Hierophant, Jesus the Christ, Who is at the head of all such brotherhoods, and it is we who desire that this information, too long hidden from them that seek truly, shall be declared openly amongst you.

Be assured there is no *human* mediator or initiator in such brotherhoods. No human head can stand the strain or possess the power. *Each soul has direct access*, and if a Teacher tells yourselves : " By this means or by that means, by my authority or by such and such an authority shall you claim admission to these sacred schools," be well assured he lies.

The Sanctum Sanctorum of each soul lies in his own centre, which is his divine spark, part of the Very GOD Himself, and only by this shall a soul enter into the wider experience of the Heavenly Temple, perfect, eternal, and all-embracing.

Truly help may be given and courage stimulated by example, but there exists no human authority betwixt the Heavenly Ones and their beloved children, the children of the human races.

In the ancient days of mystery schools, there having crept in certain abuses and certain unsuitable candidates, who knew not the ancient way of at-one-ment through initiation, these schools ceased to exist on the earth planet, but the ruling spirits of these schools were withdrawn into the inner planes, there to pursue their work unharmed by direct and unpleasing physical contact. Here the work of the soul's perfection was carried on, unsuspected by any human agencies, and as the work concerned only the higher spiritual life, it remained and flourished apart from physical intercourse.

The same methods of preparation were pursued, the same tests given, the same training insisted on, but all was carried on with the various soul candidates apart from their ordinary physical lives. Later certain occultists realized these secret brotherhoods and either joined forces with ourselves, or, in the cases of the less reputable brother-

o

hoods, they formed their own physical plane brotherhoods with ordinary physical occultists at their head.

The true test of a real mystery school is the ideal of self-sacrifice and purity of life. Any dubious occult practices at once proclaim the wrongly constituted school.

Shun them, they are spiritual plague spots ; likewise shun all who greedily seek power and high-sounding titles, they are puppets, dressed and tricked out as dolls, void of all moral worth and doomed to perish miserably.

But of all who seek God in their hearts, of all who love humanity and ever seek to raise the fallen, heal the sick, and minister to those who grieve, of such be it known there is a name writ large in blazing light upon the altar of the Great Initiator, Jesus the Christ, for hath He not said, " Inasmuch as ye do aught to the least of My brethren, ye do it unto Me."

These are they who are the members of the Inner Temple of the Most High, they who serve, not they who demand service.

Peace be unto you, my brethren.

Be it known unto you, my children, there is a ritual of service to which all may be admitted when once they have been admitted as novices or as younger brethren in the junior school of initiates ; a very high honour, to which all may aspire and to which many belong quite unknown to their waking consciousness.

Colour most exquisite, sound most wonderful, and aspirations living and intense with spiritual breath are sensed in these regions.

Do not confuse these proceedings with the ordinary experiences of the soul in its wandering in Summerland. Beautiful, restful and life-giving such as these are in that happy land, these higher experiences of the emancipated soul are beyond all these expressions.

These rituals are part of the great Cosmic expression of life on the inner planes, and it is from the pale colourless imitation of such ceremonies that the great ceremonies of the temples and churches have from time to time been taken back into the waking consciousness of mankind.

Think on these things at your own great festivals of

the year. They are ancient beyond all present-day conception.

Seek always to become one with the elect of the Heavenly Father by praise, prayer, and a desire to see God.

Peace be unto you.

THE SOUL'S AWAKENING.

There comes a time in each of your lives when your soul, like the prodigal son, lifts up its eyes from the baser desires and the more ephemeral pleasures of life, and longs, with a most distinct heart hunger, for the better understanding of the presence of God in your own hearts.

This is quite unmistakable in its longing; no longer do forms and ceremonies satisfy, all appear empty, and your spirit longs, as your scriptures say, for the presence of your Heavenly Father.

The moment this longing has taken possession of your soul, then expect many rebuffs in your search ; for at once there is a trial of your sincerity, and, if your soul still perseveres, then your soul is questioned severely before our own brotherhood as to its work, its ideals, its desire.

When your soul appears before our council, there appears also in your company your recording angel, who proceeds to give an account of your works on earth, not only in your present life, but in your past also, and, according to this history, will your desire for admission be granted or refused by us.

Happy indeed are ye if the tale of your works is sufficient to merit admission into the first school of our younger initiates, for from henceforth your lives are under special protection, and your place in the Master's service, humble or great, is at least given your soul, and your soul, however many times it may fall below its ideals, will never belong entirely to the physical and magnetic planes alone any more.

From this time the soul enters into new responsibilities, and in your daily lives frequent opportunities will arise of rendering service, either directly or indirectly, to your Master, through your fellow-beings in all stages of evolution, in all classes of life ; furthermore, your ability to deal with many kinds of activities will strangely increase ; for physical life will be much fuller of responsibilities, and your mind will begin to grow in wisdom and understanding, also in tolerance and humility. Your spiritual life will grow in serenity and in outward influence on those about yourselves.

People will tell you of their spiritual trials and seek advice, and on every side your heart will find small traces of this extension of soul experience blossoming out into your everyday life, so that no longer will your heart doubt that your soul has taken the first step, even though your physical brain may be oblivious of these actual occurrences in your soul-life on the inner planes.

Many are received into this first degree who have never even heard of the word Initiation, but one day they will know it for a fact, though probably not until their souls have passed through the portals of that experience known to yourselves as death ; it is far better in every way to come with this knowledge already firmly established in your minds, for your progress on arrival is so different, so simple ; and your hearts and minds are already familiar with ourselves, so that indeed it is a joyous return for ever from a far country, and there is great rejoicing over here.

Your work, already begun during your earth life, merely continues without interruption from one sphere to another over here—one glorious experience of spiritual growth.

Remember that every soul seeks its home in the heaven world, and the sooner it awakes to the existence of that home, the sooner will the whole community of mankind evolve towards this great and wondrous goal of spiritual life with your own Heavenly Father, who is not only your Father and Creator, but your Divine Partner.

There are many different ways of preparation, but the highest is the way of service, for each must, as your own Master Christ has said, stand amongst your fellow-beings as one that serveth. Never refuse an opportunity to serve if your soul has chosen service.

There are other ways too. The way of contemplation is usually the type chosen by the more feminine type of soul, for it is a more quiescent kind of method, and though it leads to great spiritual insight, it does not help the soul's progress so much ; it is more introspective and is not really so much use to humanity in general, but it is a very fine kind all the same. The special power of prayer is wonderful in its influence on the human beings with whom the contemplative comes into contact, but prayer must not make its devotee shrink from its fellows, this is wrong, for prayer must widen the outlook, and sweeten the soul of its special devotee.

There is the method of self-renunciation. It is a very strange way of serving, but it is through the soul's freedom from all kinds of bondage that often the soul is a kind of messenger for the furtherance of God's will on earth. It is a very distinct and often painful way, and never chosen unless the discipline of the soul demands it ; but it is a very great and fine method even though outwardly lonely. Yet remember, the soul is never alone in the spiritual realms, there is really no separation except the outward apparently physical separation in your physical life. Those whose souls have chosen this way must learn that all humanity is their tie, and that they possess an unusual freedom to exercise a peculiarly wide and general love towards their fellow-beings.

Their special line of preparation is one of general ability to initiate centres for the spread of spiritual light ; their souls are mostly practical, rather than inspirational, and hence they make fine messengers.

There is a very distinct method of service in that of healing, in which case knowledge of herbs, anatomy, magnetism, and nervous diseases, and all useful information on the subject of colour, reincarnation, auras, and so forth must be very specially studied ; this is one of the most necessary ways of serving humanity, and a method requiring a very high standard of mental and spiritual healthiness.

Now, when each soul is established in its special branch of work, then it must work steadily along those lines, and by degrees to the individual and to the individual alone, further light will be shown in due course.

Never expect advice on these points from a human head of a society ; each soul is its own saviour, and no one has the authority to dictate what the soul must do in any way ; brotherly counsel alone may be sought and given, but never, never any authority. Never make that mistake.

CHAPTER XXV

INITIATION (*contd.*)

The House of Remembrance. The Hall of Initiation. The Masonic Ritual.
Symbolic Building. Experiences in the Temple. Socialism. Passing
the Warden. Asceticism.

THE HOUSE OF REMEMBRANCE.

The House of Remembrance is the inner sanctuary of the
mystic planes of existence. It is the Great Temple of which
we are all members ; it is the headquarters, as it were, of
the White Brotherhood. It does not exist on your earth
plane, but on the higher spheres, and many are already
students and disciples in this wonderful place.

It is most wonderful in construction, for it is built upon
the great mathematical plan which is a foretaste of those
regions beyond the conception of any human consciousness
for beauty of colour, of light supernal, of sound the finest
and most soul-thrilling.

This House of Remembrance is the Temple built without
hands, created and existing in the highest Heavens. It is
not merely a figure of speech, it is indeed a place ; the
Heavenly City which has many mansions, many divisions,
many degrees of soul-development, for soul-material is the
real material of this heavenly sphere. Our own particular
House of Remembrance is the Great Hall of Initiation,
known to all those who have made the final attempt to
reach out their hands to the Great Master, for He is indeed
the Hierophant, the Master Builder, He is the One Who is
known in your own World as the Christ.

Now, when a soul has applied for admittance into this
Great Hall of Initiation, there are certain tests which must
be passed first in the outer physical, mental and spiritual
life of the soul ; and when these tests are safely passed, the

candidate is admitted in due form, and is given his own special niche in this vast Temple of Service.

All service must be freely and ungrudgingly given, or the candidate will make no advancement towards these higher degrees in the initiation rites and ceremonies.

These rites and ceremonies are regularly administered by those Hierophants in charge of the different stages of development, and these ceremonies are administered at certain seasons of the year.

Those who make proper progress are admitted by graduated steps to more and more spiritual degrees or ceremonies, but at each step there is always a halting, while the Guide makes inquiry as to the suitability of the candidate for the next step.

You can see how by degrees these ceremonies have been admitted into the brain consciousness of the human being, for all in your own Masonic ritual is only a picture—and a very dim picture it is—of the future stages of the soul's progress on the higher planes of consciousness.

This is the real meaning of initiation, and although the ordinary consciousness may, and as a rule does, remain in entire ignorance of these wonderful experiences, they are constantly being experienced by the soul, which seeks true and intelligent advancement along the Way of Attainment.

These particular methods of initiation are most beautiful, and when in your own Lodges or Chapters your ceremonies are well conducted and by a real Initiate of our own Hall of Initiation, then there is a very wonderful access of power generated in your midst, which brings the soul of the candidate into a momentary point of spiritual contact which leaves a great mark of uplifting beauty on the forehead of the aspirant or seeker.

Whenever a man desires to become a member of our own brotherhood, he is first required to give proof of his own efficiency in spiritual wisdom to our own satisfaction ; and when that has been approved, he is admitted into the first grade before he is admitted as a real member of our own inner sanctuaries.

Q. Have the physical buildings of Pyramids, Temples, Cathedrals, any actual bearing on these inner " buildings " ?

A. All Temples of whatever creed or method of religious

expression are the dense material moulds or forms of spiritual Temples, because within their exactly proportioned erections there is the recognition of certain forces in Nature which must be complied with or the building cannot remain whole.

Each type of Temple bears the symbol of the revelation of which it is the place of meeting for the people expressing that belief ; as in your own Churches the Cross is the symbol and the Cross is the usual design ; the Cross is the symbol of the revelation of the present great civilization.

It must be realized that Initiation is not a thing of a remote past, it is a matter of vital everyday occurrence, and we desire to give warning to such as will follow it that there is still a secret path of initiation leading into the heart of the mysteries of Jesus the Christ, Whose Kingdom is actually come and coming on your earth.

· · · · · · ·

In the various stages of initiation there are certain experiences to be obtained by the aspiring disciple, but no one will be accepted, however hard he struggle, until the Hierophant of each degree is perfectly certain of the candidate's readiness for admission, and his real progress in those tests already placed before him.

In your Masonic Lodges very small attention is paid to this experience because your members are really ignorant of the very real significance.

Q. Is it a fact that when people are put through the various degrees we actually put them through mystical soul experiences ?

A. It is a fact that no man can perform rites or ceremonies founded on secret wisdom and mystery teaching without setting into vibration very definite forces, occult and mystical, so that whether it is believed or disbelieved, no candidate for Masonry leaves the Temple after a ceremony without having undergone very definite soul experiences. Your members must be taught to realize this most thoroughly. The old power of the Divine Hierophant, as we knew it in the ancient mystery schools, no longer permeates your Orders, but there is instead a very powerful force generated by your action and your words, and certain spiritual or occult vibrations, very distinctive rhythms

from a higher or perhaps from an astral plane, may be
aroused and set into motion, and the candidate is unwillingly, or perhaps willingly, caught into the living stream,
and his own centres of contact stimulated wisely or unwisely, according to the power generated in a Lodge or
Chapter. Harmony must always prevail. Never participate
in a ceremony when your mind or heart rebels against its
ruler for the time being ; it is a spiritual calamity for all
concerned.

It is most essential that all those who desire to progress
by means of this particular type of teaching should have
previous knowledge of the mystery teaching of olden times ;
it is not wise to accept anyone to whom the idea is practi-
cally new or unrealized. This enables the aspirant to enter
more intelligently into the ceremony and to be more
receptive of its influences when he meets each new experience.

Let us now return to our own House of Remembrance,
for within its vast portals the whole system of mystery
teaching is sent out into the world by our own special
emissaries.

We are always working out our plans for helping and
guiding humanity, and it is wonderfully organized work.
There is no waste of energy or power, no overlapping of
office, for each member has his own work, and is known by
the colour of his garments, and the symbols he bears on his
breast.

Whenever a new soul succeeds in gaining admission there
is very great rejoicing, and all our brotherhood receives the
newly initiated soul with much loving encouragement.

At this point the soul is given more important work ;
sometimes in the helping of souls in distress on the lower
astral planes, of which there are many grades ; sometimes
in the formation of spiritual societies to teach those souls
who are young in evolution. Some are sent to those still
in human fleshly bodies ; some are used to take charge of
souls waiting to be incarnated again ; some help with those
experiments which ultimately find their way into your
material world as benefits, as discoveries, or as necessities
for progress. The inspirational part of our organization is,
as a rule, taken from the souls of all who make music in the
world of material ideas, such as poets, artists, musicians,

and inspirational writers, but much that finds its way into your earth world is not from our Hall of Learning at all, but from the grosser spirit entities who inhabit the lower mental and astral regions.

All obscene writing, painting, and all wrong music—and your music can be very wrong—all such are harmful vibrations passed into your earth plane from evil spirit entities.

Do not always condemn what your eyes cannot understand, but your intuition will tell your mind what is obscene and harmful.

Much beauty is shown in the world which is still unrecognized as beauty. This is the unfortunate cause of much misery ; there is a great need for the cultivation of beauty in all spheres of life, for beauty is perfection in form, colour, design, and in all the essentials of perfect manifestation. Do not depreciate those whose minds seek to render art manifest, however they may differ in expression. Any attempt to render an idea in concrete design is the slumbering exercise of the God faculty being awakened.

Do not be overburdened with the need of utility, but endeavour to carry artistic love into all grades and classes.

.   .   .   .   .   .

Now, when the soul has been accepted as a novice or candidate for initiation, and that is only after very careful preparation and many tests of endurance and sincerity, then the soul is taken apart into a holy place, a very special place in the inner planes. This inner place of initiation is most beautiful ; the light is most powerful, and bathes the soul in a wonderful glow of living energy and revivifies it with rays healing and purifying, so that the soul is never again without some of that inner light shining about it and helping it in all the hard tests of life in the outer planes.

When the soul has been bathed in this light supernal, it is clothed with the new white garment of the candidate, and a girdle of some fine colour is placed about the middle to denote the soul's particular grade of work or the service by which it has attained this honour.

After a rest in these inner regions, the soul is sent forth to accomplish more work with the additional advantage that this stage in initiation has given it. No human eye can carry back this picture, for the wonder of it is beyond human description, but there remains in the heart of the newly initiated brother a feeling that henceforward earthly life is only of a very secondary consideration, for eye hath seen and it hath entered into his heart some little realization of some of those things prepared by the Divine Hierophant for them that love Him and serve His people in the outer world of men.

In this Temple of Initiation the soul will meet many friends, not perhaps friends known in his earthly life, but friends known to his soul in many lives. Sometimes in this temple he will meet his lost affinity, and in such a case, there is accomplished what is known in these places as the mystic marriage of the affinities. When this is accomplished there will never be any real separation again, for the fruits of all past lives are brought to this wonderful harvest of the soul's fulfilment, and no more will these divine sparks be separated from each other ; they complete their own special life union, and the time draws near for their entire and complete union, when neither shall be sent into earthly bodies of flesh, but both shall remain on the inner planes, to work in loving unity for ever.

Now, when the soul has attained the degree of initiation into the temple, there is a period of teaching which is given by members of our own brotherhood ; it may be on occult lines, or on ceremonial lines, or on inspirational speaking and writing lines, or on public service from the inner side ; for all service which is sincerely carried out is connected with certain lines of evolution over here. Your earthly ideas of government, charity, education, and so forth, are all faint echoes of these ideas on the higher side of our own inner organizations.

All things are made in Heaven, even socialism, of which your world has such fear, but which has in its basis the real, true government of people in the best and widest sense. But these ideas are contortions on your earth plane, because they have so much to pierce through in the way of injustice and materialism, and they have contacted many evil influences in their path, which have brought about bloodshed and horrors of all kinds ; yet it is a fact, that in the distant years there will be a world socialism, a universal government, but not yet. Socialism is not a matter of a party or petty politics, but it is the conscience of the world, and any man who truly seeks the Kingdom of Heaven on earth is a socialist from the higher point of view.

There are most secret parts of initiation, which man may not enter into nor profane. These hidden places are holy, and always protected by celestial fire from those whose minds lack that degree of purity demanded by all who would enter into these secret places of the MOST HIGH.

There is a Warden who guards these portals. His name is unknown to all who wish to enter, but his work is to admit all whose hearts are pure and whose service has demanded that they be admitted. If they have power over their own bodies, if they are masters of their own five senses, if they are full of the desire for higher and more wonderful knowledge, then they are passed through this portal, by that Warden, and he is then sent to show them the hidden places of wisdom, for here the seat of wisdom is ; and knowledge of forces high and all-powerful is given these newly passed brethren, and by this wisdom alone may they approach the final stage, which makes of each an initiate or adept.

When the mind of man has learnt that such an experience as that of initiation is open to him whilst still in this human body, then there will be an advancement in spiritual matters, but at the present moment such ideas are believed to be purely imaginary, or only possible in the long past of man's physical existence. That is utterly false ; these experiences are part of your everyday life on the inner planes, but until a man makes a definite bid for this new life, then he is detained by the small physical experiences and the soul experiences are put off to some more convenient time. Your Masonic ritual is the actual picture of true happenings, yet how many know it as such ?

Q. Must we be indifferent to all human joys and sorrows before our souls can progress ?

A. This idea of ascetism is always a difficulty with those who are starting on the path of discipleship. Let us answer it as your own Master Christ answered it : " Let him that hath two coats give unto him that hath none." Never forget that your gifts of material advantages are given as tests as well as your sufferings from poverty. Riches bring responsibilitites and your own hearts must be generous in all ways of distribution of comfort. Meanwhile do not make so much of the letter of what is written, remember the spirit is much more important. Remember the teaching of those who would complain of the breaking of the rule of the Jewish Sabbath. The spirit is that which counts, not the meticulous letter of man-made laws. Law is a divine thing but there is nothing mean about it, it is wide and generous. Be ye like the Laws of your Heavenly Father, great, wise, and full of sympathy.

Q. Are those who are leading good spiritual lives yet utterly condemning all psychic matters, are they also undergoing these experiences ?

A. Not in the same way, for denial of what your brain terms psychic matters is a very great drawback, since it is a denial of truth, and truth must be recognized by all. Those who lead good and spiritual lives have their own place of development, but their progress is very incomplete, yet all their goodness must, of course, count in their favour in the final summing up. The great anti-spiritual sin is the sin of intolerance, and that is a very common failing throughout your earth plane.

Q. In the White Brotherhood is the feminine aspect of soul present ?

A. Yes, of course it is. We do not distinguish between male and female, all souls are souls, and we only think of divine emanations, not of stupid physical outward representations of men as men, and women as women.

Q. Can you tell us whether a Hierophant is a male or female soul ?

A. The Hierophant is always what your minds call a male soul ; it is, as yourself has described quite truly, the positive outpourer or initiator, and the female or negative soul is no lower but is of a different kind of functioning body.

CHAPTER XXVI

WHAT THINK YE OF CHRIST ?

Jesus the Nazarene. Jesus the Christ. Jesus the King. Woman's Responsibility.

JESUS THE NAZARENE.

The whole idea of Christianity has been confused, and made far less by the curiously twisted ideas which have been given out from time to time as the genuine teaching of the Master.

Know then, that in order to arrive at the fullest conception of this great mystery school, known as the Christian Mysteries, it will first be necessary to consider in detail the real story of Jesus of Nazareth, the Great Nazarene Teacher. This particular aspect of Jesus is the purely human one.

He was, as your scriptures tell your world, born of Mary and Joseph, they being specially chosen for their pure lives in the past, and because their vibrations would give all the necessary understanding and love necessary to a very sensitive boyhood.

At the beginning of His life there were political difficulties among the Jewish nation and the Romans, and the whole country looked for a strong deliverer from the heavy yoke under which they existed. A rumour was current that a deliverer was to be born somewhere about the time that this child made His appearance. The date is not well established, as many of your scholars are aware, and all we can tell you on this point is that the actual date is not perfectly correct, but it makes no very great difference to the ultimate history of this World Teacher.

The Jews were a well-advanced nation in the way of civilization ; they had produced good law-givers, wise kings, great prophets and teachers, and were suited in every way to produce the Great Teacher of the New Age ; but in this they failed, because when the time came their priest-hood had become corrupt, and the Great Teacher was rejected by those in authority, but was acclaimed by the more ordinary people amongst whom He had spent most of His time and healing powers.

When this child arrived, your scriptures speak of shepherds and Wise Men being aware of His birth, on account of a comet, and according to the calculations of time in the annals of the occult brethren of the day. This is more correct than perhaps many of your own people realize to-day in your own world, for such signs are always given to those who understand, whenever a new soul of surpassing magnitude is born into your earth plane.

By the law of signatures the Great Being sets His mark in your sky, and the mighty constellations bear witness of the Cosmic event which is about to take place in your midst.

This Child was not born in a stable ; that is a confusion with the language of the mystic in which the New Child or the new-born Christ-consciousness is kindled or makes itself felt alive in the inner recesses of the heart ; " in the cave " is a term known to all mystics. It does not detract from the fact that Jesus was born of apparently ordinary people, in very ordinary circumstances of living, possibly in the house of a relation, not in their own particular home.

His name had been already foretold to His Mother and Father. It had a special meaning ; it carried special responsibilities, and His life would be spent in the carrying out of these responsibilities. Thus should all names be given ; more would be accomplished by the individual if your people had sufficient knowledge to choose rightly.

This Child, as He grew, gave evidence of His very great knowledge of mystical matters ; your scriptures tell you this fact. Then the years, which were silent in your scriptures, were spent in study and in undergoing the various tests and initiations as provided in the outer and inner schools of teaching and healing, of which this Teacher became a member ; finally a great Master issued forth, and the mission began.

The issuing forth of the completed Teacher is referred to in the Baptism, as told of John the Baptist and the Master.

John was quite truly a prophet and forerunner to awaken

and stimulate the people's minds and hearts. This baptismal function was a formal taking over of this teaching from John, and was performed before certain witnesses, in order that this fact might be established.

Jesus was always a very special Spirit, because, though born in the ordinary human way, He was not on the same line of human evolution, as far as His Soul was concerned.

He was truly a Son of God ; that is, a very specially developed Soul, not hitherto incarnated in fleshly form, but provided with a pure fleshly form for His special work.

All human beings are divine, because they have received certain gifts of creation which set them apart from mere animal beings ; but there are grades or varied lines of evolution and the souls vary in degree of divinity. Jesus is of the very highest type, part of the original Godhood ; man is part of a denser kind of Godhood, more enveloped in denser matter.

Now the object of all religious teaching is to tell mankind of his inherent divinity, and to kindle in him the latent desire to return to it—for do not forget that man's fall into denser matter was the outcome of a strange Cosmic loosing of giant forces, which were uncontrollable in the beginning ; the subsequent muddle occurring by reason of the leading spirits among these forces being disunited instead of remaining in close bonds.

These points have already been dealt with by us ; we must not lose our way from the consideration of this mission of Jesus the Nazarene Master.

During His time of probation and of learning to accustom Himself to the human frame, our Master Jesus had to obey all the restrictions which human form imposed on Him, and we know that He was weary, hungry, sad, lonely, disappointed, in the same way that men suffer from these disabilities, but always in moments of prayer and of teaching, in moments of exaltation, He was fully aware of His own special Divinity and insisted that faith in Him would lead men back to their forgotten divinity.

His beautiful language was pure mysticism, and mystically true. He was and is " the Way, the Truth, and the Life," because His methods of living, loving, healing, teaching, are the true standards of divinity, and only by realizing and endeavouring to follow this standard or cross can man

hope to regain that which was lost. It is never the human
fleshly Jesus who speaks of Himself in that way ; it is the
Great Divine Spiritual Christ who points the way of attainment to the lost divinity.

"Greater works shall ye do " He said, because He knew
that man's knowledge of the laws of the unseen things
might be stupendous, "Remove mountains," to speak
metaphorically. Yet never once did He strive to make a
convert by display of his wonderful occult or secret knowledge. His interest was purely to do good where there was
suffering ; not to vaunt Himself as a worker of so-called
miracles. So that throughout His short life, your minds
are consciously led to contemplate this Man Jesus as a
Human Man, made perfect in the wonderful Love of God
immanent in the smallest as well as the greatest particulars
of existence.

Jesus the Christ was never meant to be worshipped as
the Latin peoples worship Him and His Mother and all the
various saints.

He taught first the necessity for purity of life and next
the truth of the nearness of God to each one of us. Yes,
to each one of us, for we are no nearer the Great Father of
all than you are in your own world. Your mind can very
easily grasp this great truth, because your brain knows that
there is no such distinction as place.

God is—we are—and that is the whole truth, and your
finite minds must learn to be familiar with this.

All life, physical and spiritual, is one life, there is no
demarcation at all, that is why the truth about reincarnation
should be taught.

Continuity makes life intelligible and renders that which
your people foolishly call death negligible.

When your people have grasped this, they will begin to
make proper progress.

JESUS THE CHRIST.

The Master Jesus during His life on your earth plane, was
subject in all ways to the limits of human life, but apart
from that very serious limitation, He led, and led consciously,
a far greater life of the spirit, which from time to time
showed itself in the rather more abstruse teachings which

P

led later on to a certain understandable amount of mis-understanding in the minds of those to whom only a literal rendering of His words was possible. Your mind can easily, in its moments of individual thought, call such instances to remembrance.

Throughout His divine ministry Jesus was filled with one desire—the desire to awaken in men's hearts the wonderful realization of his divinity and a strong wish to return along the path leading upwards towards the Heavenly Home, so long vacated by man's errant soul. These were the " many mansions " of which He spoke so often ; these were the states of bliss long promised by the Father to all who truly turned back to His loving partnership ; for remember man was always a partner with God in the evolution of life, and man is necessary to God for this purpose, just as God is necessary to man for the means and hope of such unbelievable glory in excelsis.

The whole drama of the spiritual life is laid bare before your own eyes in the great example of Jesus the Christ. Not only as human, suffering, aspiring man, but furthermore as the Divine Man going through a greater Cosmic life, enduring cosmically all those episodes which are part of the small human man too—birth, baptism, temptations of all kinds, marriage, death, resurrection, ascension, and triumph at the last over all.

Let us consider the Christ Birth. It is, of course, a Birth of immortal souls, not a birth of human atoms collected into the temporary mould of personality. This Birth, or manifestation in a world of form of an immortal or Divine Being, issuing from Father-Mother-God, the Immortal issue of Perfect Love, such is the idea of the Holy Child being born in a state of helplessness, dependent on the Divine Parentage, the two Cosmic forces of Love and Energy of Divine Wisdom. Here is Perfect Man as he was before the Fall and as he may be again in the ages to come ; this Divine Child of which the heaven form is the immortal spirit, and of which the earth form is the helpless infant. The heavenly child is born in the heart, in the secret cave, in man's inner consciousness ; but His Body is not of this world, it is of the spirit everlasting and primordial, great beyond all understanding. This child may be born in your own hearts, when the chamber is prepared, and love and

wisdom are engendered and established therein, as the
Divine Parents of this Divine Child.

The naming of this child is important too, for at this
mystic rite the name that proclaims his future work is
given, the name by which His Heavenly Father will call
Him to give account of His lessons during that life.
" Thou shalt call His name Emmanuel—God with us."
Herein lay the wonderful mission of Jesus the Saviour, the
very personification of God in your very midst.

The teaching, the school life, the various vicissitudes
of youth and adolescence are all passed through like various
initiations, until the great day of baptism or the entry into
the new life of ministry, teaching and healing, helping,
serving, and saving, the lot of every true Son of God, whether
of Jesus the Christ, or of one of your own humble selves.
Remember the significant washing of the disciples' feet.
He washed their feet as a token of loving service and purification of the lowest physical members of their physical body.
He made reference to this task as a symbol of service,
meaning that when a man seeks the higher life, not only
must his own members be clean and undefiled, but he
must be willing to render any kind of service for his
fellows.

Then the temptations, their significance, then the Feast
of Remembrance.

Now this Feast of Remembrance is a most important
part of the life mystical, because it is actually part of a
very great experience in the inner planes, when, during a
certain part of your earth year there is enacted in the
higher states of consciousness a very wonderful ceremony
amongst all those who have learned to understand what
this Sacrament really means.   No blood-rite this, but a
joyous remembrance of the beautiful unity and immanence
of God behind all manifestation, whether on your own
earth, or in these heavenly regions.

When each of you has definitely set out on the path
leading to eternal life in this Heavenly World, then your
soul receives certain garments of purity—your heavenly
confirmation garment ; and just as in your own Church
life your boys and your girls are blessed and received into
the Church as members on their own merits, so with your
more developed soul consciousness, your reception into this

body, mystical of divine union with the spiritual forces, the soul is received into the midst of a vast concord of souls seeking the fulfilment of this aspiration.

None is sent empty away, and none may enter without this white or wedding garment of personal purity and dedication.

The ancient mystery schools taught this, and taught their novices how to contact this inner life with conscious knowledge, whilst still in their purified mortal bodies. The way lies open to all, even at this present time. Jesus the Christ showed, was and is, the Way, the Truth, and the Life. But not by self-immolation may your freedom be bought, that is by the immolation of the Divine Man Jesus, but only by your own efforts and by your own character building in your own earthly life.

This reception into the higher consciousness bears on its wings the further responsibility of certain ceremonial experiences—for the soul has to meet its own special mate, the affinity from whom sometimes it has long been separated ; the Heavenly Bridegroom seeks the bridal soul, the Divine Bride seeks the aspiring Bridegroom. " In My Father's House there is neither marriage nor giving in marriage," is a fine truth, greatly misunderstood in your world, where marriage has become a feast of carnal appetites, rather than soul-mating and spiritual union. Truly there is no marriage or giving in marriage, for in this heavenly state the soul affinities are knit into one perfect whole or divine marriage, and love in its highest and best similitude is the accepted ideal of unity. All who have loved well, all whose lovers are in these higher regions, all meet in a great and perfect union, where sex is a law of perfect union, and not a manifestation of physical opposites.

Jesus the Christ is spoken of as the Heavenly Bridegroom of the Church ; this is in a measure true, but not the Church as she stands to-day, rent with schisms, dogmatic, full of foolish strivings after pomp and power and non-spiritual details. The Bridegroom demands love at its highest, fullest, and most perfect ; not quarrels, bitterness and mad striving for favour.

In Jesus the Christ and His perfected Church your minds must behold the reunion of the great affinities of Love made perfect in a marriage of spirit and form, of which each soul,

male and female, will one day be also examples in the higher
spiritual realms of the heavenly life eternal.

Much has been written of the Death on the Cross, the
pathetic figure of a tortured Christ has been held up to your
gaze for many centuries.

I say unto you, not so must your hearts regard the
Saviour of the world, the Saviour or Servant of humanity.
Truly death was His portion, but this emblem of the Cross
is not the sad, bloodstained standard of human degradation ;
it is a glorious standard of service and of courage and of
the perfect union of Spirit and Form—divinized form—the
meeting on the central pivot where the arms cross of the great
Cosmic forces of a far greater entry into the fleshly emblems
of the human body.   Think of the form of MAN perfect and
archetypal, standing with outstretched arms, free to
embrace, free to serve, free to uplift all who truly turn to
Him, the pattern of all time.   That is the true Cross of
Christ, the true emblem of the Saviour, the symbol of " God
with us."

The Crucifixion was a human tragedy, the Cross of Christ
is a divine symbol of joy and realization.   Honour the Man
Jesus for His martyrdom, but glory in Jesus the Christ for
His greater life of spiritual truth laid bare for the understanding of those who care to read this vast mystery with
the light of their own mystical knowledge.

The second portion of the story of Jesus the Christ is the
great mystery of your Christian Church, so strangely mis-
interpreted by your own teachers and preachers from the
beginning until this present time on your earth plane.

Now, this mystery is one which is no mystery at all
to those whose eyes are accustomed to look beneath the
surface of mere outer symbol—those whose hearts catch the
beautiful vision of the Cosmic Christ, Great Universal Love
Spirit throughout the ages, for that is what the Christ-
consciousness is—the fulfilling of the Law, that is, the Law
of Love.

Your mystic Paul has set all this plainly before your eyes :
" Love never faileth," he wrote, and truly love shall never
fail in the end.

It is the doubting minds of men which seem to cause it
to fail, but only on the surface.   There is a fundamental
love, which is, after all, the only law by which life becomes

coherent and possible—first the rhythm of number, the creative force of uttered sound, made intelligible to your human minds by the understanding of this first law. Then the rhythm of form, proportion, beauty made manifest on your own planet, from ideas set into rhythmic motion on the higher plane of Divine Ideation. Then rhythmic motion, the breathing into sentient existence the Breath Divine, causing individuality and power hitherto appertaining to the Great Logos.

Then the extension of the rhythm between all life in all planes, just as a living garment of love, perfect order, perfect and complete harmony between the three aspects of creation, body, soul, and spirit, whether of the Divine Godhead, the Trinity, or whether of the body, soul and spirit of human man, or whether of the body, soul, and spirit of the universe ; all interpenetrate with harmony, and Divine Love is the Medium of all understanding, so that these three trinities are united as a symbol of the complete Cosmos.

At this point it will be necessary to turn to the subject of the glorious Resurrection and Ascension to the higher Heaven World of the Man Jesus of Nazareth.

It is understood that this Jesus of Nazareth was killed and that His Body was laid in the tomb prepared for Joseph of Arimathea ; here all precautions were taken against any attempt to pretend that a miracle had occurred. There was no need for fear, the Body of this Perfect Man was of different substance in this way—that It could not see corruption, It was dissolved or re-absorbed into the original elements and His soul and spirit bodies released from this Sheath which had rendered Him visible to ordinary human beings.

Side by side with this laying in the tomb of human death is the laying in a trance state of the subtler bodies of this advanced Initiate ; and during this temporary rest of this outward or fleshly body, The Master Jesus ascended into the highest planes on His last Initiation Rite. Hereafter He was free of the earth planet, His work accomplished, His entire victory over all the physical and spiritual trials accomplished.

The Resurrection of Jesus the Christ is an event of vast importance, because it does prove that death is nothing at all but a passing state. He returned and carried on His

ministry for some long time, although the fleshly envelope
had disintegrated.

Your own bodies of the flesh will never resurrect ; there
is a great loosing of the fleshly sheath which becomes part
of the original mother earth, and your soul and spirit bodies
may use a pictorial wraith at times to make your presences
recognized to those on earth after this loosing, if there is a
special need for this reappearance ; but as a rule there is
no need, and the body of the flesh sinks into the coarser
atoms of the earth, and the ego, the real living personality,
leads its free life on other planes, bound only by its own
desires, the desire for a re-birth, or the desire to serve, or
the very necessary task of fresh knowledge obtainable in the
heaven worlds.

The so-called ascension into heaven of the Master Jesus
was no fresh experience, and was not an event of any
particular day or hour. He lived in the Heaven World,
and had free access, but from that particular event your
minds were taught that there is a permanent home eternal
into which all may one day ascend, and where there will
be no further issuing forth into this particular world of
yours, when the earth incarnations are finished, and the
soul with its shining garment and its new name walks a
citizen of the New Jerusalem, the City of God the Heavenly
Father. Here higher work claims the newly freed soul, and
all restrictions of fretting limitations are gone for ever.

This, then, is the great and glorious future for each human
soul, but it is a state not easily won, only the reward of
unselfish living, of purity, striving, and of a genuine desire
for the treasures of heaven above all the illusory phantoms
of physical pleasure and gratification.

JESUS THE KING.

The subject will now deal with the third aspect of our
Master Jesus, King of your world to come, and by this we
mean the Kingdom of God in the hearts of men, for just as
in the early days of His life on earth He was regarded as a
potential King, and in mockery was slain as a pretender
to the throne of Israel, so in truth He is to be regarded in the
future as the King of your earth, in the sense that in the
golden age to come His standard will be the standard

raised aloft for the salvation of mankind. By the Cross and all that it means will mankind slowly climb upwards towards a far higher ideal of perfect understanding of his own place in the universe, and by the realization that only through the adoption of the higher life taught and lived by Christ Himself will it be possible for man to regain his own long-lost Kingdom.

Now, when your minds regard this Man Jesus as a purely human man, your minds lose sight of the incomparable glory of His Sonship of God the Father. Your teachers and preachers are not really aware of it, they stress too much the idea of a dying Saviour, but though the Man Jesus died a tragic death, it is as an *undying* monarch that your hearts must do homage to Him.

The real difference between these two aspects of Jesus as the Christ and Jesus as King lies in the very truly mystical import of the Kingdom of God on earth. That is a fact which you never understand, that Jesus is really King of your present rising civilization, your own special Race Teacher, Preacher, and King.

The King of the world is some type of Being whom your minds have not learnt to understand or appreciate. It is a very special position, which over here we understand entirely. In these realms we recognize a Being, the King of the planet on which there is life closely resembling free human beings, whom we designate by the sign or symbol of Kingship, as well as we can explain this term to your own world.

In olden times the human idea of Kingship was something divine ; the King possessed unusual powers of occult knowledge, although he was then a human man in the ordinary sense of the word ; but he held his kingship by reason of certain advancement in his incarnations, and on account of his being able to contact the secret forces more perfectly, as in the case of the Kings of Egypt ; they were Priests, Kings, and Initiates of the real order of Melchisedec, a most wonderful school of Initiates, known later on to the Jewish initiates also.

These half-divine, half-human beings, were empowered with many great gifts, and hence arose the idea that a king had divine rights and could cure all kinds of diseases and perform miracles.

This state of affairs did not last so very long, owing to the abuse of powers ; that is generally the reason for these gifts disappearing for long periods of years, but this particular position being a reflection from the higher planes of certain aspects of divine government, so there exists this particular type of ruler, known, as it would be in your language, as King.

Every new great civilization has in these higher realms a mighty Being who is the ruler over all the planes of that civilization, that is, its mental, spiritual, and physical embodiment. At present your King over your own world civilization is this same Jesus the Christ ; the Cross is His Symbol, and the great law of love and self-sacrifice is the ideal to be engendered in that particular civilization, a new commandment given unto you that ye love one another.

Once this law is fully established on your earth plane, the Kingdom of Heaven is already established in your midst. Do not believe those who say your civilization is as evil as those that went before. Already there are signs throughout your world that your people strive towards this wonderful ideal. Many who say these things have no real sense of the real Brotherhood springing to life in your cities.

There is to-day a quickening of man's consciousness. He knows he must help his less fortunate brother, and above all this stupid luxury and desire for sensation there is a steady striving for the betterment of the human man, woman, and child. The very frictions between your several organizing bodies, your schisms, your international attempts to promote purity of life, food, health, and government, are all splendid signs of life, but no one must rest contented to allow others to work. Work, service, these are the tools ready to your hand, nor seek to lay them down until the end of your lives on earth. Each worker is needed in his own special quarry or business or profession. Each of your women must yield her special gift of the mind, the heart or the body, for on woman depends the future of your civilization.

She must demand life at its best for her children, these little ones so full of potentialities of this great future. Never must she make light of the special burden laid upon her throughout all time.

Woman is the cradle of the race ; her womb holds it,

her soul inspires it, her love suffers for it, shields it, and again reproduces it. It is a mighty heritage; never let her eyes lower their gaze from this celestial vision of her responsibility towards the perfecting of the man, who is (whether male or female in outward physical appearance) the partner of the Great Being whom ye call God.

This then, my children, is to be the work of the immediate future—the work of preparation for the coming golden age. Work on, we are with your minds and souls and bodies in all brave and unselfish endeavour. But remember, only by selfless striving for the highest, only by letting this Man Jesus stir the loving devotion in your hearts, only by raising His blessed standard aloft in your lives, only by letting this Jesus the Christ be born mystically in your spiritual lives, only by acknowledging Him as the King awaiting His welcome in your midst, can your whole being be raised to this perfection of the measure of the Stature of Christ, King of all the earth, High, Omnipotent, Gracious and Loving Monarch for ever and ever.

CHAPTER XXVII

THE CHRISTIAN MYSTERIES

The Christ-Drama. Birth. Naming. Baptism. The Ministry. Temptation. Crucifixion. Resurrection and Ascension. Vicarious Atonement. The Feast of Remembrance.

BIRTH.

The Mystic Birth has already been suggested in the
instruction given by ourselves on the subject of Jesus the
Christ, and each soul, as it arrives at this stage of individualized knowledge of itself (that is, when it arrives at the
point in its evolution when, even in the human body, it is
conscious of that divinity without any shadow of doubt),
then is it born in the midst of outer darkness, " in a cave,"
in a sanctum sanctorum, the divine and ineffable being
which is born of a " pure virgin," conceived in love and
divine knowledge, to be " a light to lighten the Gentiles,"
or the outer senses of the human personality.

This is the first step of the soul's pilgrimage through the
Mysteries of the Christian school—the divine birth.

NAMING.

Next there is the naming of the child or young soul, and
this name is actually bestowed in the inner planes, and
corresponds to the naming of that special line of development which is to be the destiny of this soul in this particular
life-expression on the physical plane.

It may be in the way of service, healing, teaching, saving ;
in preaching, in ruling, in initiating ; in expressing beauty
or wisdom through poetry, art, music ; in colour, form, or
sound ; but each soul receives its name, and it responds to
that name, and this response vibrates to a certain chord
or note of one of the strings of development.

It is not always easy for the soul to learn its name or its work, because many lives, lived in ignorance, often make this knowledge difficult to impart, but perseverance and determination, and, above all, faith in the great destiny of each soul will one day result in this hidden knowledge being unveiled to the seeking soul, so that when the actual drama of the soul is in full swing, as it were, the naming of the young child is heard and understood.

It follows that the naming and showing forth of the particular line of soul-development to be followed will necessitate long years of education, and it is then that the discipline of school life begins, and the soul learns its lesson throughout life, and the various classes which, knowingly or unknowingly, the soul attends.

BAPTISM.

The great event of public baptism follows—the washing in the eyes of witnesses, the dividing of the life into a new channel, when the soul steps out of the river Jordan, and departs on its new work of ministry and of homeward turning—for all wisdom and understanding have been accorded and gained, and the soul is as one having authority, a true teacher and ministrant of the mysteries of God the Father.

THE MINISTRY.

There follow next three years, three periods of the soul's ministry ; the healing of the physical needs of the fellow-beings ; the teaching of the outer wisdom for the multitude ; and the inner teaching for those whose soul development is sufficiently advanced to receive this inner teaching.

Do not be mistaken in this. In every soul this takes place ; it is the ordinary line followed by each in turn, as the soul becomes ready, so that, in effect, the humblest may indeed follow in the footsteps of the Master Jesus, and, in His own individual way, may lead just such a life of ministry in whatever circumstances that soul may be placed.

" Take up thy cross and follow Me " ; that is no idle tale, no pretty imagery of speech ; the cross is the emblem of cosmic origin, the union of spiritual verity with physical manifestation, and man must lift it freely and carry it boldly, understanding its joyous significance ; for his own body is the standard, free, erect, with arms extended to help and uplift, to praise and glorify.   How thrilling this thought, freedom and again freedom ! Freedom of choice, freedom of love to serve, freedom of light to express.

TEMPTATION.

So then the ministry is entered upon, and the soul nears its release from physical rebirth.   But first the tests—the wilderness and hunger ; the exceeding high mountain and ambition ; the pinnacle of the temple and spiritual pride. Body, soul, and spirit, each is tested in turn, and when these are finally rejected, then the devil leaveth temptations, and angels appear and minister unto the soul which has won its own release from all temptation.

From this point the soul enters on a very different life ; hitherto the life has been in the physical body, on a physical plane with human or physical limitations ; but from henceforth the soul ascends into a far greater or higher degree of consciousness.

CRUCIFIXION.

Here comes the true crucifixion, for the cross no longer is the symbol of the soul ; it has transcended it ; it sleeps upon it, dies, as it is put in your own scriptures ; and after strange wanderings in the inner planes, is raised into a body everlasting, eternal, incorruptible, and never again to be born in physical form.

RESURRECTION AND ASCENSION.

The soul has returned to the Heavenly Father ; the marriage feast has been given, the soul is united to its own affinity, the ring of union is placed upon the finger, the spotless robe has been put on, the new and more glorious name bestowed and it shall go out no more.

The soul is free of all planes of existence, it can ascend and descend at will, it is resurrected and ascended into Heaven, it may sit at the right hand of God the Father, whose Kingdom has no end.

This, then, my children, is your future, your great triumph ; no idle dream, but the great aim, end and goal of your existence, from which none may be turned away but by his own persistent will for evil.

This, then, is the summing-up of the mystery of Christian teaching ; and just as Jesus the Christ has trodden all these ways before your own eyes, even so may each soul rise from the darkness of sloth and of ignorance, and turn again, like the prodigal son, eyes of longing and heart of desire towards the Home that is afar off, where there will be ecstasy of rejoicing over each soul that decides to be born anew and travel back over the long road that leads Home.

VICARIOUS ATONEMENT.

Now, my children, there are certain errors which are current in your world to-day, which have done much to impede the progress of those who desire truth. Never believe that any vicarious suffering on the part of this Jesus can ever save your soul from the pains and penalties which it deserves. There is a measure of forgiveness of sins, it is very true, but this only releases the debt against the human creditor, it does not free the soul from its own debt to humanity in general. Whatsoever a man sows that he must reap, and though repentance helps him against committing that sin again, yet must that sin be wiped out in a fitting manner which life shall serve out to him.

THE COMMUNION SERVICE.

Your Feast of Remembrance is no feast of forgiveness, nor of vicarious suffering ; it is a cosmic feast, well known in all schools of mystery teaching.

The earth gives of her body to nourish man, and man labours in harmony with Mother Nature to produce that nourishment ; and just as he is formed of his mother, so his mother nourishes him and all his brethren, and in that common brotherhood he recognizes a common parentage, and verily by the eating and drinking of the earth-mother's body and blood, he partakes of a mystic communion of his Divine Father and Mother, through whose cosmic union he alone has emanated into a physical existence.

The symbolism is cosmic, beautiful beyond all earthly expression ; he is part *of* his mother, part *of* his father, and part *with* his brother-man. This is the great cosmic mystery of the Presence or Immanence of God in all things ; and as God is to the Universe, the Divine Husband to the Divine Wife, so is Man to both—the Divine Son : body of their eternal body, and blood of their all-pervading blood or life-essence.

CHAPTER XXVIII

THE NEW AGE

The New Teacher. Public Worship. The Feast of Remembrance. Service of Healing. Meditation Services. Church Design. The Great Winnowing. Priesthood. The Ancient Order of Melchisedech. The Duty of the White Races.

THERE is a new life awakening in the world of the future, when much that is now evil will be at peace, and all the present wars and rumours of wars, strife of all kinds, petty jealousies, racial differences, sex antagonism, cruelly wrongful feeling towards God's creatures in other states of evolution, will be quiescent and Man will arise to greet the new dawn of life in the new age, which will be patiently waiting to greet this awakening of souls ; a new age is even now dawning in little suspected corners of the world from West to East, from North to South.

The New Age will be very productive of men and women who were once in your world at the time of Jesus Christ, for a man will be born into the world who will be a very marvellous Being, and the world will then be much readier for him then than it is now.

That is why we desire certain teachings first to prepare men's minds to develop along the right lines. We must help the world to be able to benefit by the teaching we will impart to all who make up their minds to receive Him as the Great Teacher who will be due then.

This concerns the Priesthood as it must be in the future ; for the present Priesthood has lost the true mystery, or inner teaching of your own Teacher, Jesus the Christ. He is the King of the new dispensation, and His teaching will be revealed by a new teacher in the next few years, for his Master is also Jesus the Christ. He will bring newer and richer teachings to help those who truly desire the Heavenly

Kingdom upon earth. This is no idle prayer, but one of deepest significance.

Now when this new age shall dawn, there will arise in the midst of your own people a new desire for worship of the most exalted spiritual kind. They will desire anew that worship shall be a thing of emotional, spiritual, and intellectual beauty ; all emptiness of form and ceremony will fail to satisfy, for men will, by that time, have learned that rites and ceremonies are not mere repetitions of platitudes and prayers, but they will know far more of the effect of certain specialized actions in ceremonial, which will stimulate their soul-bodies into a far greater rhythmic appreciation of spiritual forces.

The intellect must be cultivated together with the emotions and the spiritual intuitions ; only so will the highest type of religious endeavour ever be able to realize the immense splendour of worship as a body united in a single act of homage.

That is how we understand worship, and it must never pander to mere emotionalism ; the crude ideas prevalent in your churches to-day are a travesty of the divine homage such as is fit to be offered to your Heavenly Father.

The chief service will be the old Feast of Remembrance, such as we hold in our own Temple of Initiation.

Wine and Bread or Cake, the Sacramental offering of the Body of Nature, offered as a link between Nature who provides it, man who labours for it, and the Lord of Heaven Whose Love and Will have given Being to Nature, Man, and their sustenance.

It is indeed a Love Feast, as well as a Feast of Remembrance, and all in taking it must learn to realize that no man lives by bread alone, nor by wine alone, but by inspiration of the Lord and Giver of Life whose infinite foresight has made Himself, Man, and Nature of one Body, spiritual, cosmic, physical and human.

It is this sacrament wisely broken, poured out, administered and partaken, that makes the bond between the different parts of the Great Trinity, making of them a wonderful unity, for so indeed shall man realize that as God, the Great Being of all Beings, becomes part of His own Creations, so man, by eating and drinking of these simple symbols of God's Creation, verily eats and drinks of the Body and Blood

Q

of the Great Being of all Beings. This is not a bloody sacrifice of a human body as a propitiation for sins, but something infinitely nobler and worthier than this terrible idea, an idea founded centuries later by crudely ignorant priests, never left as this by Jesus the Christ, Who knew only too well the beautiful significance of this sacrament of Bread and Wine.

All Initiates have known this truth through all the ages, and Jesus in uttering these words was merely using these words as the Hierophant of that particular mystic Feast of Remembrance which they were celebrating before His own cruel murder.

His death was a noble example of complete self-surrender, but in no sense was it a propitiation for the sins of the world, and no Heavenly Father was ever concerned in the unhallowed demand for His blood.

The next very important part of the new church services will be the Service of Healing, for this long lost gift of spiritual laying-on-of-hands in the process of healing must be restored without delay. It will be seen who among the people and the priests possess the power or gift of healing, and gradually this will be brought back into the religious side of life, and those who can heal will be drawn into that special side of Church Service. This will not eliminate all doctors and surgeons, for they will gradually be drawn into these ranks, for many of your wisest medical men are healers now, did they but understand it. Many will be healed of very serious ailments and accidents.

There will be stated periods of time for Meditation Services, and very special leaders will be found, who will help to lead the prayers of the people along the wisest and most spiritual channels. People will search the scriptures diligently ; they will not listen sleepily to idle repetitions of what are, so very often, deep mystical words.

Inspirational speaking and writing will be recognized as part of the genuine teaching, and there will be a wise direction of the psychic faculties when they are discovered in a person.

There will be a very special design of Church in the future, which will be constructed on a different plan.

There is a very great winnowing at this time ; the wheat truly is being separated from the chaff, and it is all to serve the wonderful purpose of the future.

Stand firm, for we all need your small bodies of sound and honest endeavour, they shine through the world's darkness, and wherever we see these lights, there we show forth our power in every way.

Great will be the knitting together of all such material later on, and then the real progress of the future spiritual Kingdom on earth will be established.

We said that Healing, Teaching, Meditation, were to become very special branches in the new Church and this is indeed the truth ; but no doubt your minds ask the question why are these matters considered signs of a new dispensation ? They are not really new at all ; they have been the actual ideals of all great religious teachers in turn ; and in turn each has tried to carry out a proper system which lays just these principles before those whom the system tries to help, guide and instruct.

Yet in turn each system fails, and each new system starts afresh, with ever the same longing to find God in its own special way.

Man has always instinctively sought his God, but he often loses all sense of the nearness and of the all-pervading love of his God, because he allows certain powers of priestcraft to make divisions between God and himself.

You see how even religion reincarnates, for each fresh system is only the Great Soul of God incarnating in a new material form for the soul of man to emulate and follow.

At this time you are beginning to rebel against what is termed by yourselves priestcraft and dogmatic teaching. This is perfectly natural, because priestcraft and dogma have betrayed your trust, and folly has raised creeds which —though often very true in their mystical sense—are so incorrectly taught and believed in, that the more intellectual among your people turn from them.

PRIESTHOOD.

Yet do not turn from priesthood. It is a geniune form, established for the true guidance of your own souls by the Great Being whom your hearts recognize as God.

There are three orders established in the higher spheres to help in the ruling, guiding, and teaching of your own people on your own earth plane. They are the offices of Prophet, Priest, and King, and all perfect government recognizes these groups.

We are concerned just now with the priestly order, the Ancient Order of Melchisedech, for this is that order created from the beginning of human evolution to teach those who need it, that their souls may find, in ceremonial, help and teaching, a great force for contacting the higher or inner regions of the soul. The priest, the true priest, holds the cure of souls in his charge, if he be worthy of his great calling. But ceremony often is no more than a shadow of the real thing, and contact is lost or enfeebled, and the true power of the priest ceases to exist in the higher spheres, and is only a vain shadow of the real office.

Pomp and desire for personal advancement have always meant the downfall of all that is great in the human being. The priest is the servant of his divine Master, a mere steward of these high mysteries ; yet often is he a self-seeker and an unspiritual cumberer of divine offices.

The Order of Melchisedech is the most ancient of all orders, even older than the Brotherhood of whom your Guides are all members, but this order exists for the purpose of teaching to men the truths of priestly service, for all priests who are worthy of that high office are of this ancient Order.

The use of ceremonial is threefold ; it makes the forces of the higher planes become attracted to the special body using this ceremonial ; it also contacts the hidden occult centres in a man's body, and it brings about a very fine vibration of occult force of the very highest kind in the case of spiritual mediums, and only such really spiritual mediums are genuine members of our Order.

Now when in your own midst there is a particularly spiritual medium, it is very possible to contact one of our Order, without the medium being actually a priest as your orders regard such priests.

Now, of a truth, there are many points which need explanation. The spirit of the scriptures needs understanding rather than the actual wording, for the story of certain incidents has been confused and often badly rendered by faulty scribes.

In order to understand true Christianity it is necessary to understand all great religions, all mysteries, all the various branches of ancient wisdom teaching.

Your minds are obsessed by this terrible sense of separation ; there is no separation of divine wisdom ; it is all one vast fount of spiritual outpouring from the hearts and minds of those bright spirits sent by the goodness of the King of your earth planet, your Heavenly Father (to use a kindlier term) to help mankind in its upward struggle towards perfection and union with its own Divine Progenitor.

Crude, bestial, hateful indeed have many of these teachings become through the distortions of man's own evil or undeveloped mind, but the root of all God-sought knowledge, the foundation of all God-given wisdom, is always the divine planning of a universe so vast, so beautiful in design, so marvellous in its carrying out, so worthy of all homage and love, that the ultimate conclusion of each individual soul is that of humble adoring love and desire for a more perfect knowledge of the Great ONE I AM.

Unity has descended into diversity, and diversity aspires towards unity, that is the fundamental idea at the root of all religious thought.

Teach men to realize this, and the bond of a world's brotherhood is already forged in chains of living gold.

Teach men to understand the intermingling of their souls with the souls of the universe, and of the dependence of both on the Great OVERSOUL which is GOD, and they will never sin against the higher self within them.

Herein lies the work of the White Races, to cultivate the intellect of their people, to feed them with spiritual food, not foolish dogmas, by telling them how to reach out to God, and how to contact all spiritual forces by their own efforts, through prayer, meditation, and the gifts of the spiritual faculties.

CONCLUSION

RECEIVED IN WILDERSWYL, SWITZERLAND. MAY 28th, 1929.

THE object of this later revelation to the world, given through the hand of our servant, your present writer, has been to enable all those whose hearts yearn for a real glimmering of Divine Truth to illumine their hearts, to find within these lessons something of that ancient wisdom of your own Heavenly Father which the ages have hidden under a veil of superstition and of misrepresentation.

Never again will this Light be entirely quenched, for many of those who read these words will hear the inner voice of their own higher self calling distinctly and even commandingly to them to arise and set forth on the path which leads to the life eternal, immortal, and above all human understanding.

Let these words sink into your own subconscious minds, remembering that your minds are only functioning in your everyday life with a very small ray of development, in a very limited human body, and that the Great Divine Consciousness, perfect, complete, and all-understanding, is held prisoner by those fetters, often deliberately and foolishly forged by your puny human brains, which are not aware all the while of that great and glorious being, which is your real self, made in the image of your Divine Father, your Partner, your own beloved Creator and Progenitor.

My children, read these pages and find in them truths which all the while exist for your own hearts to find. No knowledge is hidden from those that truly seek ; no prayer remains unanswered by those who watch your every endeavour to find God Himself.

No one walks alone ; none suffers alone ; none is cast out into an unfriendly chaos to fight and struggle unheeded or unwanted.

All are necessary to the Heavenly Father ; all are wanted by your own Great Master Jesus the Christ, whom ye serve very often blindly, unwittingly, and unconsciously ; for He is ever in your minds and in your hearts, watching your lives, caring for your own small trials, loving each small service, whether rendered in His name or in the name of your own common humanity, or in the service of all those creatures which have been set in your own midst.

Take His messages of love literally, as they were meant. He will not leave your minds or hearts comfortless ; He is ever in the midst, whenever two or three are gathered in His Holy Name.

Remember all that has been said of the great doctrine, or rather, the great truth of reincarnation, for it is a profound message of evolution in all phases of existence, whether cosmic or human, and only so will your minds be able to appreciate the immensity, the perfect justice and the exact adjustment of all life, in all your experiences and in all your knowledge of these profound laws of your own universe.

There is one law of life, one law of all religions, one law cosmic, universal, and one law human and divine—the Law of LOVE—all-pervading, all-permeating, omniscient and omnipotent, and only as man rises to heights truly glorious and unimaginable will his eyes be opened, and his ears unstopped to this great music of the Eternal and Ineffable I AM, whose first great desire for the expression of His own great Force of Love gave to all manifested creations their beauty in form and in divine ideals.

The soul is its own saviour, and its own initiator into the higher realms of spiritual realization. By slow and often most laborious means, it climbs the spiral of its individual evolution, and none may interfere to hinder or to help. Only loving counsel may be given by those that have passed that way before them.

None may wipe off the sweat of toil but he that toils. None may taste of the bliss of cooling streams from holy fountains but he who has toiled faithfully and loyally.

None may rest in those many mansions, which are indeed prepared for all who labour in the field of earthly harvesting, but he who has borne the burden and heat of the earthly day, the day of physical incarnation.

There are always helpers at your side ; there are always helpers in your own realms or spheres ; and we who once laboured and suffered in your world of sorrow and of wonderful training, greet you and tell you that we are ever in close communion with such of you as turn towards this higher life of the soul.

Behold we are always with our brothers in the flesh, even as your Master, the Great Jesus, is ever in the midst of your spiritual endeavours.

The veils lift, the clouds are pierced by the first gleams of a coming dawn.

We, who love you, greet you in the Name of our GOD, and in the Love of our Christ, and in the Fellowship of our White Brotherhood.

INDEX

A

ABSENT TREATMENT, 154, 161
Adam, 124
Æsthetic training, 199
Affinities, 21, 188
Air, 82, 90, 97, 99
Amethyst (colour), 169
Amulet, 176
Anger, 71
Angle, solid, 84
Animals—
  Astral plane of, 45
  Reincarnation of, 191
Ankh, 87
Antagonism, 187
Ascension, 237
Astral entities, 70, 73
Astrology, 77
  Freewill, 77
  Horoscope, 78
  Law of Periodicity, *ib.*
  Planetary influences, 77
Attainment, way of, 134
  Clairaudience, 142
  Clairvoyance, 141
  Contact at Séances, 148
  Diet, 147
  Direct voice, 142
  Divine quest, 134
  Evil practices, 144
  Materializations, 143
  Mediumship, 138
  Mediumship trance mediums, 149
  Mediumship type required, 146
  Names, difficulty with, 140
  Prayer and Meditation, 135
  Spirit-photography, 143
  Spirit-writing, 139
  Testing writing, 141
  Time, difficulty with, 140
Atonement, vicarious, 30, 238
Attraction, law of, 81
Aura, 106

B

BAPTISM, 236
Birth, 22, 235
  Control, 133
Blood, 115
Blue (colour), 168
Body. *See* Man
Brotherhood, white, 67, 214
Building, symbolic, 38

C

CENTRE, 19
Chaos, 48
Christ. *See* Jesus Christ
Christian mysteries, 235
— Baptism, 236
— Birth, 235
— Crucifixion, 237
— Ministry, 236
— Naming, 235
— Remembrance, feast of, 238, 241
— Resurrection and Ascension, 237
— Temptation, 237
— Vicarious Atonement, 238
Church design, 242
Circle, 40
Clairaudience, 31, 142
Clairolifactoriness, 31
Clairsentence, *ib.*